"*Beyond Reengineering* is an exceedingly coherent statement of why process focus is a powerful way to think about a business. . . . The ultimate compliment for [this book] is that I look forward to rereading it and will urge my colleagues to read it as well."

—Peter B. Lewis, CEO, Progressive

"Michael Hammer challenges us all to confront the radical changes that process-driven corporations are bringing to individuals and to society. It is the breadth of that challenge and the depth of his insights that make this book everybody's business."

—Robert Allen, Chairman and CEO, AT&T

"Dr. Hammer provides a practical, 'real life' discussion . . . and shows us the reward for kicking bureaucratic habits that still get in the way of serving customers."

—Ed Crutchfield, CEO, First Union

"Michael Hammer's new book is an important step in the continuing journey into a process-centered world most of us know very little about."

—Wayne Calloway, Chairman and CEO, PepsiCo

"I strongly recommend *Beyond Reengineering* to learn how companies can organize for learning, value creation, and sustainable growth."

—Robert S. Kaplan, Arthur Lowes Dickinson Professor of Accounting, Harvard Business School

D0981036

BEYOND REENGINEERING

HOW THE PROCESS-CENTERED ORGANIZATION IS CHANGING OUR WORK AND OUR LIVES

MICHAEL HAMMER

HarperBusiness
A Division of HarperCollins*Publishers*

A hardcover edition of this book was published in 1996 by HarperBusiness, a division of HarperCollins Publishers.

BEYOND REENGINEERING. Copyright © 1996 by Michael Hammer. All rights reserved. Printed in the United States of America. No part of this book may be used or reproduced in any manner whatsoever without written permission except in the case of brief quotations embodied in critical articles and reviews. For information address HarperCollins Publishers, Inc., 10 East 53rd Street, New York, NY 10022.

HarperCollins books may be purchased for educational, business, or sales promotional use. For information please write: Special Markets Department, HarperCollins Publishers, Inc., 10 East 53rd Street, New York, NY 10022.

First paperback edition published 1997.

Designed by Irving Perkins Associates

The Library of Congress has catalogued the hardcover edition as follows:

Hammer, Michael, 1948–
    Beyond reengineering : how the process-centered organization is changing our work and our lives / Michael Hammer. — 1st ed.
       p.   cm.
    Includes bibliographical references and index.
    ISBN 0-88730-729-9
    1. Reengineering (Management) 2. Organizational change. 3. Industrial organization. I. Title.
    HD58.87.H36   1996
    658.4'063—dc20   96-10718

ISBN 0-88730-880-5 (pbk.)

00 01 ❖/RRD 20 19 18 17 16 15 14 13 12

In memory of the innumerable members
of the Hammer and Gartner families who perished in the
Holocaust, especially the grandparents I never knew,
the aunts and uncles and cousins I never met,
and the rest of an extended family of which I was never
a part—but whose influence I feel every day.

CONTENTS

Acknowledgments

Acknowledgments are the most difficult part of a book to write: it is hard to know where to start and even harder to know where to stop. At the very least, however, I must express my appreciation to the many colleagues and collaborators who contributed to the development of the ideas in this book, especially Steve Stanton and Bob Morison. I owe a special debt of gratitude to Donna Sammons Carpenter, both for her editorial help and for continually challenging me to improve and refine and extend my thinking. Many individuals contributed to the research, editing, and production processes, including Tiffany Winne, Phil Bodrock, Erik Hansen, Susan Buchsbaum, Pat Wright, Cindy Sammons, Elyse Friedman, Martha Lawler, Richard Lourie, Sebastian Stuart, and Maurice Coyle. Without Hannah Beal Will's orchestration this book would never have seen the light of day. Bob Barnett, as ever, provided wise counsel and effective representation. On the personal side, I owe more than I can express to my wife, Phyllis, and to our children for their patience and encouragement: their equity in this project is high indeed. The greatest credit of all, of course, belongs to those progressive men and women who are leading the revolution in business that this book describes; many of them are named herein, but many are not. To them go both my thanks and my admiration.

FOREWORD

THIS BOOK is not about reengineering; it is about reengineering's consequences, about its aftermath and its abiding legacy.

In the second half of the 1980s, a handful of companies—Ford Motor Company, Texas Instruments, Taco Bell, and a few others—embarked on programs of business improvement that would transform American industry beyond recognition. Faced with unrelenting global competition and ever more powerful and demanding customers, these companies came to realize that their old ways of operating—their long-standing methods for developing, making, selling, and servicing products—were no longer adequate. They also discovered that their existing tools for improving operations were not making a dent in persistent problems of high cost, poor quality, and bad service. In order to address these problems, these companies had to take measures more radical than they had ever taken before. Forced to choose between sure failure and radical change, they opted for the latter. They began to reengineer. They ripped apart their old ways of doing things and started over with clean sheets of paper.

The good news is that these extreme measures, born out of

desperation, succeeded far beyond anyone's expectations. These pioneering companies and the many others who followed them achieved breathtaking improvements in their performance. As word of their success spread, reengineering became a mass phenomenon, a vast global business movement. Only the willfully ignorant or those with private agendas question the impact that reengineering has had on businesses around the world.

However, some bad news followed this good news. In the aftermath of reengineering, business leaders discovered that they no longer understood how to manage their businesses. Reengineering had not just modified their ways of working, it had transformed their organizations to the point where they were scarcely recognizable.

The source of this dislocation was to be found in a modest and unassuming word in the definition of the term "reengineering." Since I first coined that term in the late 1980s, I have consistently used the same definition for it: Reengineering is the radical redesign of business processes for dramatic improvement. Originally, I felt that the most important word in the definition was "radical." The clean sheet of paper, the breaking of assumptions, the throw-it-all-out-and-start-again flavor of reengineering—this was what I felt distinguished it from other business improvement programs. This also turned out to be the aspect of reengineering that captured and excited the imagination of managers around the world.

I have now come to realize that I was wrong, that the radical character of reengineering, however important and exciting, is not its most significant aspect. The key word in the definition of reengineering is "process": a complete end-to-end set of activities that together create value for a customer. The Industrial Revolution had turned its back on processes, deconstructing them into specialized tasks and then focusing on improving the performance of these tasks. Tasks—and the organizations based on them—formed the basic building blocks of twentieth-century corporations. The persistent problems companies faced in the late twentieth century, however, could not be addressed by means of task improvement. Their problems were process problems, and in order to solve them companies had to make processes the center of their attention. In taking this momentous step, corporate leaders were doing more than solving a set of vexing performance problems. They were bringing down the curtain on close to two hundred years of industrial history.

By bringing processes to the fore, reengineering turned organizations ninety degrees on their sides and caused managers to take a lateral, rather than a vertical, view of them. This shift has obviated the certainties and prescriptions of management textbooks. Virtually everything that has been learned in the twentieth century about enterprises applies only to task-centered enterprises, the hitherto dominant form of organizational life. For a world of process-centered organizations everything must be rethought: the kinds of work that people do, the jobs they hold, the skills they need, the ways in which their performance is measured and rewarded, the careers they follow, the roles managers play, the principles of strategy that enterprises follow. Process-centered organizations demand the complete reinvention of the systems and disciplines of management. This book is a report on the early stages of this endeavor, a first draft of a business guide for the twenty-first century.

Beyond Reengineering is about the present as it becomes the future. It is not a book of speculation and imagination; it is based on observation and projection. The concepts and techniques we explore are all in use today. Tomorrow is not around the corner; it is already in our headlights.

Although this book had its origins in reengineering, its lessons are not limited to companies that have formally embraced reengineering. Some companies approach process centering by taking the high road of reengineering while others take the winding path of total quality management. Both the inhibitors and the determinants of business success in the global economy are process issues, and only process-centered companies will be in a position to deal with them. Any organization that hopes to thrive in the twenty-first century must reach the destination of process centering.

In a sense, what follows is a prospectus for a series of books. Each of the topics we examine here—from work life to business strategy to the requirements for sustained organizational success—deserves a volume, or a set of volumes, of its own. I have tried to outline the broad themes of work and life in the process-centered world, but much more remains to be understood and to be written on all of these topics.

Four major themes are addressed in this book. Chapters 1 through 4 are called "Work"; they examine the nature of process-centered work and what it means for the people who perform it. "Management" is examined in chapters 5 through 9: the new role and nature of the managerial activity. Chapters 10 through 13 concern themselves with "Enterprise," the issues that must shape the agenda of twenty-first-century business leaders. The last three chapters, "Society," explore the effects of process-centered organizations on the lives of all who live in societies based on them.

This is a business book, but it is a book for everyone. We are all business people. Calvin Coolidge's often-mocked statement that "the chief business of the American people is business" was in fact very wise. Business is everyone's concern, for business is not merely the domain of profit and loss, of buying and selling, of stocks and bonds. Business is about productive economic activity, about doing work that creates things of value to others. Anyone who works lives in the "business world." Business is about getting things done; it occupies a central place in all our lives.

Business not only pervades our lives, it shapes our thinking and our words. The language of business is not just a technical argot used by specialists. We all speak of work and workers, of management and managers, of jobs and organizations. "Businesslike" is a term of high approbation. The ideas of modern business shape how we look at the world and how we see ourselves in it. Yet the language of modern business and the basic ideas on which it is founded are undergoing profound change. Before long it will be as quaint to speak of workers and managers and jobs as it already is to speak of knights and squires and quests. The radical transformation of work has ramifications far beyond the walls of the factory, the office, and the stock exchange. Business is the seed that forms the crystal that is our society. As the seed changes, so does the crystal. The process-centered organization is creating a new economy and a new world.

The road to process centering awaits the leaders of organizations prepared for the journey. This book will, I hope, help to illuminate their path.

PART I

WORK

CHAPTER 1

THE TRIUMPH OF PROCESS

REVOLUTIONS OFTEN begin with the intention of only improving the systems they eventually bring down. The American, French, and Russian revolutions all started as efforts to ameliorate the rule of a monarch, not to end it. Reform turns into revolt when the old system proves too rigid to adapt. So, too, the revolution that has destroyed the traditional corporation began with efforts to improve it.

For some twenty years managers of large American corporations have been engaged in a relentless effort to improve the performance of their businesses. Pressured by suddenly powerful international (especially Japanese) competition and ever more demanding customers, companies embarked on crusades to lower costs, improve productivity, increase flexibility, shrink cycle times, and enhance quality and service. Companies rigorously analyzed their operations, dutifully installed the newest technological advances, applied the latest management and motivational techniques, and sent their people through all the fashionable training programs—but to little avail. No matter how hard they tried, how assiduously they applied the techniques and tools in the management kit bag, performance barely budged.

The problems motivating managers to make these efforts were not minor. The operating performance of established corporations was grossly unsatisfactory, especially when compared with that of aggressive international competitors or hungry start-ups. Some cases in point:

- Aetna Life & Casualty typically took twenty-eight days to process applications for homeowner's insurance, only twenty-six minutes of which represented real productive work.
- When buying anything through their purchasing organization, even small stationery items costing less than $10, Chrysler incurred internal expenses of $300 in reviews, sign-offs, and approvals.
- It took Texas Instruments' Semiconductor Group 180 days to fill an order for an integrated circuit while a competitor could often do it in thirty days.
- GTE's customer service unit was able to resolve customer problems on the first call less than 2 percent of the time.
- Pepsi discovered that 44 percent of the invoices that it sent retailers contained errors, leading to enormous reconciliation costs and endless squabbles with customers.

This list could be extended indefinitely. The inefficiencies, inaccuracies, and inflexibilities of corporate performance were prodigious. This was not a new phenomenon; it was just that by 1980 these problems were starting to matter. When customers had little choice and all competitors were equally bad, there was little incentive for a company to try to do better. But when sophisticated customers began deserting major companies in droves, these problems rocketed to the top of the business agenda. The persistence of performance problems in the face of intense efforts to resolve them drove corporate leaders to distraction.

After a while, understanding gradually dawned on American managers: They were getting nowhere because they were applying task solutions to process problems.

The difference between task and process is the difference between part and whole. A task is a unit of work, a business activity normally performed by one person. A process, in contrast, is a related group of tasks that together create a result of value to a customer. Order fulfillment, for instance, is a process that produces value in the form of delivered goods for customers. It is comprised of a great many tasks: receiving the order from the customer, entering it into a computer, checking the customer's credit, scheduling production, allocating inventory, selecting a shipping method, picking and packing the goods, loading and sending them on their way. None of these tasks by itself creates value for the customer. You can't ship until it's been loaded, you can't pack until it's been picked. A credit check by itself is simply an exercise in financial analysis. Only when they are all put together do the individual work activities create value.

The problems that afflict modern organizations are not task problems. They are process problems. The reason we are slow to deliver results is not that our people are performing their individual tasks slowly and inefficiently; fifty years of time-and-motion studies and automation have seen to that. We are slow because some of our people are performing tasks that need not be done at all to achieve the desired result and because we encounter agonizing delays in getting the work from the person who does one task to the person who does the next one. Our results are not full of errors because people perform their tasks inaccurately, but because people misunderstand their supervisor's instructions and so do the wrong things, or because they misinterpret information coming from co-workers. We are inflexible not because individuals are locked into fixed ways of operating, but because no one has an understanding of how individual tasks combine to create a result, an understanding absolutely necessary for changing how the results are created. We do not provide unsatisfactory service because our employees are hostile to customers, but because no employee has the information and the perspective needed to explain to customers the status of the process whose results they await. We suffer from high costs not because our individual tasks are expensive, but because we employ many people to ensure that the results of individual tasks are combined into a form that can be delivered to customers. In short, our problems lie not in the performance of individual tasks and activities, the units of work, but in the processes, how the units fit together into a whole. For decades, organizations had been beating the hell out of task problems but hadn't laid a glove on the processes.

It wasn't surprising that it took managers a long time to recognize their mistake. Processes, after all, were not even on the business radar screen. Though processes were central to their businesses, most managers were unaware of them, never thought about them, never measured them, and never considered improving them. The reason for this is that our organizational structures for the last two hundred years have been based on tasks. The fundamental building block of the corporation was the functional department, essentially a group of people all performing a common task. Tasks were measured and improved, the people performing them were trained and developed, managers were assigned to oversee departments or groups of departments, and all the while the processes were spinning out of control.

Slowly and even reluctantly, American corporations began in the 1980s to adopt new methods of business improvement that focused on processes. The two best known and most successful were total quality management (TQM) and reengineering.

Through a long period of intensive application of these techniques, American businesses made enormous headway in overcoming their process problems. Unnecessary tasks were eliminated, tasks were combined or reordered, information was shared among all the people involved in a process, and so on. As a result, order of magnitude improvements were realized in speed, accuracy, flexibility, quality, service, and cost, all by at last attending to processes. The application of process-oriented business improvement programs played a major role in the competitive resurgence of American companies and the revitalization of the American economy in the 1990s.

So far, so good. But to paraphrase an infamous statement from the Vietnam era, process-centered improvement techniques saved companies by destroying them. By bringing processes to the fore, the very foundations of the traditional organization were undermined. A disregard for processes had been built into the structure and culture of industrial era corporations. The premise on which modern organizations were founded, Adam Smith's idea of the specialization of labor, was in fact a rejection of process. It argued that success was based on fragmenting processes into simple tasks and then resolutely focusing on these tasks. By attending to processes instead, the new improvement efforts created stresses that could not be papered over.

Who would have control over the newly recognized and appreciated processes? Consisting as they did of diverse tasks, processes crossed existing organizational boundaries and thereby imperiled the protected domains of functional managers. The new ways of working did not fit into the classical organization. They often entailed the use of teams, groups of individuals with various skills drawn from different functional areas. But such teams had no place in the old organizational chart. Whose responsibility would they be? The new processes often called for empowered frontline individuals who would be provided with information and expected to make their own decisions. This was heresy in organizations where workers were considered too simple to make decisions and where the need for supervisory control was considered a law of nature. In short, it quickly became clear that the new ways of working that marvelously improved performance were incompatible with existing organizations: their structure, personnel, management styles, cultures, reward and measurement systems, and the like.

There were only two options: Abandon the new processes that had saved the company or adapt the company to the new ways of working. The choice was clear, albeit difficult and, to some, unwelcome. The death knell was ringing for the traditional corporation. In its place would arise a new kind of enterprise, one in which processes play a central role in the operation and management of the enterprise: the process-centered organization.

No company adopted process centering as an end in itself, or because managers thought it would be interesting, exciting, or fashionable. Companies did it because they had no choice, because they could not make their new high-performance processes work in their old organizations. This transition began slowly in the early 1990s with a handful of companies like Texas Instruments, Xerox, and Progressive Insurance. Since then, the stream has become a flood. Dozens of organizations are now making this change, and hundreds more soon will be. Companies like American Standard, Ford, GTE, Delco, Chrysler, Shell Chemical, Ingersoll-Rand, and Levi Strauss, to name just a few, are all concentrating on their processes.

The change to process centering is not primarily a structural one (although it has deep and lasting structural implications, as we shall see). It is not announced by issuing a new organizational chart and assigning a new set of managerial titles. Process centering is first and foremost a shift in perspective, an Escherian reversal of foreground and background, in which primary (tasks) and secondary (processes) exchange places. Process centering, more than anything else, means that people—all people—in the company recognize and focus on their processes. This apparently modest and simple shift has endless ramifications for the operation of businesses and for the lives of the people who work in them. Before we begin to examine these, let's examine why process is such a departure for Industrial Age corporations.

We can think of a process as a black box that effects a transformation, taking in certain inputs and turning them into outputs of greater value. Thus order fulfillment basically turns an order into delivered goods. It begins with an order from the customer that describes a need and ends with those goods in the customer's hands. In fact we might say that the order fulfillment process creates three outputs: the delivered goods, the satisfied customer, and the paid bill. The surest indication of a satisfied customer is the paid bill. This latter, seemingly obvious observation is revolutionary. It says that the operational work of order fulfillment goes beyond mere inventory handling and shipping to include billing, receivables, and collections—the activities needed to actually get cash in hand. These latter activities have traditionally been the sanctified province of the finance department. To suggest that they should be linked with operational activities in a common process and that the line between operations and finance should consequently disappear defies one hundred years of corporate theology.

Product development is another process encountered in many organizations. It takes as input an idea, a concept, or a need and ends with a design or a functioning prototype for a new product. Many kinds of people participate in the product development process. Research and development (R&D) people contribute technical expertise, marketing people offer their knowledge of customer needs, manufacturing experts say what can be produced efficiently and economically, and finance people assess whether a product can be made and sold at a profit. The difference between product development on the one hand and R&D on the other is central: The former is a process whereas the latter is an organizational unit, a department comprised of technical and scientific personnel.

People from R&D are needed in processes other than product development. In many industries, from electronics to chemicals, R&D people participate in the customer service process. When customers call with complex questions about sophisticated technologies, the technical people are the only ones who can respond. In other words, processes transcend organizational boundaries. Xerox executives discovered this when they constructed a simple matrix diagram. Across the top they wrote the names of their processes, down the side went the names of their departments, and in the squares of the matrix an X went to any department involved in the performance of the corresponding process. When the diagram was complete, they were astounded to discover that nearly all the squares were Xs. Virtually every department was involved in virtually every process. This is the moral equivalent of saying that no one had any responsibility for anything. Or to put it another way, everyone was involved, but with a narrow focus on the activities of their own department, and so no one had end-to-end responsibility.

It is important to realize that companies moving to process centering do not create or invent their processes. The processes have been there all along, producing the company's outputs. It is just that heretofore the people in the company were unaware of their processes. People on the front line and their direct supervisors were so focused on their specific tasks and work groups that they could not see the processes to which they contributed; most senior managers were too removed from the fray to appreciate processes. So the processes have always existed, but in a fragmented, invisible, unnamed, and unmanaged state. Process centering gives them the attention and respect they deserve.

Most managers are blind to the performance of their processes. I like to ask them such simple questions as: How long does it take your company to conduct such and such a process? What is its accuracy rate? What is the degree of customer satisfaction with it? What is its cost? The answers are almost always hopeless shrugs of the shoulders. Managers can offer huge amounts of performance data on tasks and departments, but not on processes, which are the very heart of the entire enterprise. Everyone is watching out for task performance, but no one has been watching to see if all the tasks together produce the results they're supposed to for the customer. At the end of the day, the question has always been, "Did you do your job?" So the warehouse maximizes inventory turns, shipping focuses on shipping costs, the credit department assures that credit standards are met. But no one asks, "Did the customer get what was ordered, where it was wanted, and when we promised it?" So long as workers did their jobs, the result for the customer, it was assumed, would take care of itself. Nothing, of course, could have been more wrong.

Process centering changes all this by altering the perspective of an organization. As always, language is key in shaping how people view the world. We have said that a process is a group of tasks that together create a result of value to a customer. The key words in this definition are "group," "together," "result," and "customer."

A process perspective sees not individual tasks in isolation, but the entire collection of tasks that contribute to a desired outcome. Narrow points of view are useless in a process context. It just won't do for each person to be concerned exclusively with his or her own limited responsibility, no matter how well these responsibilities are met. When that occurs, the inevitable result is working at cross-purposes, misunderstandings, and the optimization of the part at the expense of the whole. Process work requires that everyone involved be directed toward a common goal; otherwise, conflicting objectives and parochial agendas impair the effort.

Processes are concerned with results, not with what it takes to produce them. The essence of a process is its inputs and its outputs, what it starts with and what it ends with. Everything else is detail.

Another commonly encountered process reinforces this point: order acquisition. At first blush, "order acquisition" sounds like consultant mumbo jumbo. There ought to be, one would think, a clear, monosyllabic, red-blooded, American word for this process—namely, "sales." In fact, "sales" does not do at all. "Sales" is, first of all, a word that most organizations use for a department full of sales representatives; it denotes an organizational unit, a department. But even more seriously, it identifies only one of the many activities involved in the process of acquiring an order from the customer. "Order acquisition," in contrast, indicates the desired outcome, the purpose of the process—namely, getting an order in hand. The difference between the two terms is the difference between mechanism and outcome, between means and end.

The single most important word in the definition of process is "customer." A process perspective on a business is the customer's perspective. To a customer, processes are the essence of a company. The customer does not see or care about the company's organizational structure or its management philosophies. The customer sees only the company's products and services, all of which are produced by its processes. Customers are an afterthought in the traditional organization: We do what we do and then try to sell the results to customers. But a process perspective requires that we start with customers and what they want from us, and work backward from there.

A process approach to business is particularly appropriate today, for we are living in the age of the customer. For most of industrial history there were more buyers than things available to be bought. Companies were limited by production capacity, not by market demand. Though not technically monopolies, many industries behaved as though they were and took their customers for granted. This is no longer the case. Today, customers have ever more choices and they are very aware of them. A company that does not resolutely focus on its customers and on the processes that produce value for its customers is not long for this world.

The time of process has come. No longer can processes be the orphans of business, toiling away without recognition, attention, and respect. They now must occupy center stage in our organizations. Processes must be at the heart, rather than the periphery, of companies' organization and management. They must influence structure and systems. They must shape how people think and the attitudes they have.

Some companies convert to a process focus in dramatic fashion. For instance, on January 1, 1995, American Standard, the $5 billion manufacturer of plumbing products, heating and air conditioning systems, and truck brakes, totally converted itself to a process-centered philosophy. It abolished old titles, realigned management roles, instituted new measurement and reward systems, and implemented a host of other changes consistent with a process view of the company.

This approach is relatively rare. To begin to focus on its processes and become "process centered," an organization need not make official pronouncements, need not issue a new organizational chart, need not employ the term "process centered," need not go through any formal procedures whatsoever. It merely has to start behaving in a different manner. Most companies join the process revolution in a decidedly low-key and evolutionary fashion. Managers and workers alike simply start paying attention to their processes, and eventually all aspects of the company are realigned with this new perspective.

To be serious about its processes, to start down the road to process centering, a company must do four things. First, the company must recognize and name its processes. Every company has its own unique set of business processes. Earlier we mentioned order fulfillment, product development, and order acquisition as representative processes found in many different companies. But these are not universal, nor are they the only processes that companies have. Most enterprises discover that they have a relatively small set of key processes—typically between five and fifteen—but their identity depends on the company's industry and the key results it produces for its customers. "Market selection," "provide after-sales support," and "develop manufacturing capabilities" are examples of other processes I have encountered. Obviously, no small number of such processes will suffice to completely describe the work of a business. Often companies divide primary processes into a small number of subprocesses, which are then describable in terms of basic tasks or activities.

The identification and naming of a company's processes is a critical first step, and not one to be taken casually. It requires rigorous care to ensure that real processes are being identified. This is difficult because processes cross existing organizational boundaries. A rule of thumb is that if it doesn't make three people angry, it isn't a process. Many organizations fool themselves by simply relabeling their existing functional units as processes. Process identification requires a new cognitive style, an ability to look horizontally across the whole organization, as if from the outside, rather than from the top down.

The second key step is to ensure that everyone in the company is aware of these processes and their importance to the company. The key word is "everyone." From the executive suite to the shop floor, from headquarters to the most distant sales office, everyone must recognize the company's processes, be able to name them, and be clear about their inputs, outputs, and relationships. Moving to a process focus does not immediately change the tasks that people perform, but it does change people's mind-sets. Process work is big-picture work.

One company where everyone appreciates its processes is Hill's Pet Nutrition, the division of Colgate-Palmolive Company that manufactures and sells animal nutrition products under such brand names as Science Diet. In the old days, if someone approached a worker on the Hill's manufacturing floor and asked what he did, the worker would have said that he was operating a machine. If the machine was running and he was meeting his daily quota, then he felt he was doing his job. If the output of his machine piled up, that wasn't his problem. If the product didn't get shipped, that wasn't his problem either.

If you ask the same question today, the worker will say that he works in the production subprocess of the order fulfillment process. Is this just new corporate jargon? Not at all. It represents a refocusing of the individual and his activities from the small to the large.

Now the worker realizes that he is not there merely to do his own thing, to run his machine. He's there to contribute to the overall effort, namely to perform the process that leads to the result of shipped goods. Now, if his output piles up, he will take it upon himself to see what's happening further down the line. He will do this not out of company loyalty, but because his sense of who he is and what he does has been reshaped by the shift from a task to a process orientation.

We have already remarked on the importance of language in any fundamental change in perspective. The Industrial Revolution not only turned peasants and artisans into factory workers, it practically created the term "workers" to describe them. Today this term, with its narrow task connotation, is dead language; it doesn't fit as we move to a process focus. Instead of (task) workers, we must speak of (process) performers, people who understand that in doing their work they are contributing to the performance of a process.

The third step to process centering is process measurement. If we are to be serious about our processes, we must know how well they are performing, and that means having a yardstick. Companies must identify the key measures by which each of their processes will be assessed. Some of these measures must be based on what is important to the customer. By studying customers and their requirements of the output of the process, a company can decide whether to measure cycle time, accuracy, or other aspects of process performance. Another set of measures must reflect the company's own needs: process cost, asset utilization, and other such typically financial matters. Measures are essential not only for knowing how the process is performing but for directing efforts to improve it. The converse of the old saw "that which is measured improves" is "that which is not measured is assuredly in the tank."

Whatever measures are employed, they must reflect the process as a whole and must be communicated to and used by everyone working on the process. Measures are an enormously important tool for shaping people's attitudes and behaviors; they play a central role in converting unruly groups into disciplined teams. "Team" is also an important word in process-centered organizations. Unfortunately, it has been much used and abused of late. A team is not a group of people who work together, or like each other, or share opinions. A team is a group of people with a common objective. The same measures for all performers of a process turn them, no matter where they are or how diverse they may be, into a coherent team. Some processes may be performed from beginning to end by individual performers, but, as a rule, processes are performed by teams.

The fourth step in becoming serious about processes is process management. We have already seen how the shift to a process focus began when companies applied process-focused improvement techniques to persistent performance problems. These efforts began the process-centering revolution; but process centering is a revolution that, like Trotsky's, must be permanent. A company must continue to focus on its processes so that they stay attuned to the needs of the changing business environment. One-shot improvements, even dramatic ones, are of little value. A process-centered organization must strive for ongoing process improvement. To accomplish this, the company must actively manage its processes. Indeed, we can now see that the heart of managing a business is managing its processes: assuring that they are performing up to their potential, looking for opportunities to make them better, and translating these opportunities into realities. This is not a part-time or occasional responsibility. Attending to processes is management's primary ongoing responsibility. Process centering is not a project, it is a way of life.

These four steps start an organization on the road to process centering, but they are not the whole journey. Process centering is a fundamental reconceptualization of what organizations are all about. It permeates every aspect of the business: how people see themselves and their jobs, how they are assessed and paid, what managers do, the definition of the business, and, ultimately, the shape of the societies that depend on these organizations. In succeeding chapters we will explore each of these themes, but let us start with the heart of the matter: the people in a process-centered organization and the work they perform.

CHAPTER 2

VOICES FROM THE FRONT LINES (I)

THE TRANSITION to process centering does not occur in the rarefied atmosphere of corporate boardrooms. The real action is on the front lines, where people who do the real work of the business redirect their thinking and change their behavior. Every corporation implements process centering in its own way, and every individual is affected differently. Nonetheless, there are common patterns in what process centering means to people, even across apparently different environments. We will now hear from three people who have made this transition. They are frontline workers in companies that followed the reengineering road to a process-centered destination. These people will not talk to us about the theory and concepts of processes. They will tell us about the realities of working and living in entirely new ways: not just what it means, but how it feels.

DEBORAH PHELPS OF SHOWTIME

In 1991 Showtime Networks decided that it had to reinvent its billing and collection processes. The old system was costing Viacom Inc., the owner of the Movie Channel, Showtime, and other premium cable-TV channels, $10 million a year in direct write-offs and even more in lost sales.

In the cable-TV industry, operators of local cable systems buy programming from companies like Showtime. The contracts generally call for the cable operator to pay a fee for each customer who uses a particular service. The cable operators keep the tallies of subscribers and calculate the monthly payments. Showtime's audit department would check the subscriber tallies and payments, but it got around to only about a third of its clients each year, so errors could drag on and compound themselves over as many as three years. A $15,000 mistake could grow to more than half a million dollars over thirty-six months. As a result, it wasn't unusual for Showtime's financial department to phone customers and tell them that they owed several hundred thousand dollars in back fees. This, naturally, led to disputes that Showtime often settled by writing off some of the charges—to the tune of about $10 million a year, or 2 percent of its revenue.

But the $10 million a year was only a small fraction of the true cost of Showtime's poor billing practices. Since angry clients weren't eager to buy new services, sales representatives wasted time soothing ruffled feathers and straightening out misunderstandings when they should have been out selling more services. Something had to be done.

Before Showtime's transformation, Deborah Phelps was a collection representative in the credit department. Today she is a financial service representative, leading a process team that handles everything from writing contracts to collecting payments to answering customers' questions.

Before, I handled a portfolio of regional accounts. I kept track of whether customers were paying us on time. If there were problems, I'd call them. But if they said they didn't owe anything, I'd do the paperwork and have it signed off by my supervisor, who had it signed off by the director, who had it signed off by the vice president.

If it wasn't the right amount, I didn't worry about that. I was just concerned about whether it was on time. In fact, I didn't even know if it was the right amount; I didn't have enough information to know that. I just knew whether we got a check for January's license payments. That was all I did.

The accounts receivable department worried about whether it was correct. It would come to their attention when their data-entry clerks entered the payment. If something came up on the screen that looked inappropriate, the data-entry clerk would take it to his or her supervisor, who would take it to the manager, to the director, and on and on. There was no group of people who actively understood what the contracts and deals entailed, or who could speak with affiliates to correct the situation.

It was a very hierarchical system—very rigid and very traditional. I had a manager; I reported to him. He reported to the director, and the director reported to the vice president. At no point would anyone speak to anyone else unless they were directly above them. You really had to follow the chain of command. For the first year, I didn't think my department head knew who I was because we never spoke. It was the classic organization where you didn't cross any lines and you spoke only to the person you reported to.

Other people in my area also did collections, but we had no interaction. They didn't work on my accounts, and I didn't work on theirs. I might go to them to find out how to process a certain form, but they had no knowledge of the specifics of my accounts. It was just me and my boss.

Then, in June of 1992, Showtime's chief financial officer, Jerry Cooper, and the CEO, Tony Cox, held a town meeting about how the company was hurting itself with some of its business procedures. They focused on how our system of auditing payments often resulted in arguments with the clients and in settlements that essentially threw money out the window. They also pointed out how we irritated clients when they called us by transferring them all over the place. That was true. I only did one function, so if someone got my name because I was helpful, I couldn't help with anything else because I didn't know what was going on.

The executives did a presentation on these problems and on how we had to improve the relationship between our own financial department and the sales staff so we could become more customer-service oriented. At that point, they introduced the concept of reengineering. I'd worked for another organization that operated in team mode, and I remembered how rewarding it was. I thought it was wonderful that they were going to do it here. Then I was lucky enough to be selected to work on the pilot project.

It couldn't have come at a better time for me. Before that, I was pretty bored and thinking about leaving Showtime. It's a really creative company, but it was rigid. I felt like I was in a box.

My team was myself, someone from accounts receivable, and a couple of people from audit. We moved from the accounting area to another part of the building. There was a real team sense to it. It wasn't like, "This is my job and I'm not interacting with other people." When I think back on all my work experience at Showtime, this was probably the most exciting time for me.

The first thing we did was to cross-train each other. I had to learn how to interpret our contracts, how we billed customers, and how they paid. I learned that it wasn't enough for a customer to send us a check, I had to understand whether the payment was correct. That was a big piece. Until that point, I didn't understand the deals and contracts. I also had to understand a little about what our auditors do. And I had to have a more global sense of our business, which I didn't have until then.

We also had liaisons with field sales. They met with us and talked about contracts and about what they did.

The biggest piece of our work was to identify what happened in our different work areas, then figure out how to make it work better. We looked at the whole audit process—accounts receivable, collection, credit, and billings—and we tried to figure out how a team of four or five people could handle all those functions and eliminate the handoffs. Our goal was to make it one-stop shopping for our field sales people as well as for our customers.

The team was very participatory, not at all like the old hierarchical system. I felt that what I thought counted and that our leader rolled up his shirtsleeves to work with us. In a hierarchy, you're not party to a lot of what's going on because it's behind the scenes. In this environment, pretty much everything was on the table.

Within the team it took us a while to figure out how we were going to work. We were told there were no rules, to think "out of the box" and be as creative as we could. Maybe for the first week or two, I thought, "Do they really mean that?" Then I just went for it, as did some other people. I felt we'd been given this golden opportunity. But some people held back.

After about six months we took the pilot program department-wide. There was a town meeting led by the chief financial officer and the new head of the financial services department, Tom Hayden. At that session, Tom answered questions about what would be happening with everyone's job. He also set a time to meet with every person in the department for a half-hour talk about their concerns and what they'd like to do in the organization.

When we introduced the new plan, some people thought it was really exciting and challenging. But others never quite understood it and were resistant. The implementation phase has been difficult for a lot of people. Some weren't able to adapt and had to leave the company.

When the program was first rolled out, I applied to be a

team leader. But I wasn't chosen, so I became one of four financial account specialists on a team that was based in New York, but with a leader in Denver. Because the leader wasn't in the same office, it called for a lot of initiative from the team members. I ended up assuming a leadership position because I took more initiative than anyone else on the team.

If a problem came up, I suggested we get together as a team and propose a solution rather than just calling Denver and asking for one. I think I was pretty instrumental in pulling the team together for meetings on a regular basis. There were also a lot of meetings among the leadership team—all the team leaders. Since our leader was in Denver, I was always called in to represent my team. This gave me a lot of information firsthand that I shared with the rest of my team. I tried to solicit input and opinions from everyone as often as possible.

There's been a lot of reshuffling of the teams since we first put them together. Eventually, it was decided that the team leaders had to be in the same location as the teams. I was promoted to be a team leader, and I moved to Chicago, which was the area we serviced. Normally, the team does the hiring of new members. But in this instance, I was the only one left on the team, so I basically hired the two new people. I looked for people with high energy and experience in the industry. The two people I eventually hired came with impeccable references from the Chicago office. I thought it would be a real ace in the hole if I could come in with people who already had contacts and had proven themselves in Chicago.

At a recent training session in New York, we did some team-building exercises and talked about our goals. We looked at the department's vision statement and wrote a vision statement for our team. I think people are starting to feel that the company's goals and objectives are theirs rather than something that was just handed down. We've also looked at areas we thought we need to work on.

On my team last year, one difficult issue was taking initiative and taking full ownership of the work. When we went through our organizational shake-up, a number of people were asked to leave. Most of them had been with the company for a long time. I think they'd become comfortable and weren't used to going the extra mile. They were told they had to take more initiative and participate more. That's not a problem on our team now; there's a lot of initiative and risk taking.

Another important thing about teams is that your work really affects the other members. So we have had to learn to give feedback and deal with each other. It's really difficult to try to change behavior, but it can be done. One person on our team didn't respond until her teammates started giving her direct feedback. She hadn't paid much attention when she'd been getting direction from her boss because she figured that the supervisor "doesn't know what I do anyway." But when she heard the same thing from four members of her team, she really took it to heart. She was offered assistance in getting up to speed, and she took it. People would say, "What do you need? What gets in the way of your following through?" And she'd work on learning.

For example, she wasn't very well trained in the accounts receivable process, so our expert sat down with her and went through the whole system while she took notes and asked questions. I think she came as far as she did because she had a real desire to be with the company, and although she was struggling, she saw the benefits of the new work style. I think there were people who didn't care and didn't see any benefit in trying to change.

Under the team system, there's no place to hide and eventually everything becomes apparent. In New York there was this really nice person that everyone liked, but we were finding all these mistakes. After a while, other members of the team got frustrated at the work that wasn't getting done right and the extra time they had to put in. It caught up with him. When we did a reevaluation of the organization, we were told to look at performance, not personality. People were really honest, and he came up short.

Another thing that's changed in our new, flatter organization is that you have to look at the whole concept of promotions differently. It's no longer about achieving the next level, it's about increasing your skills set and getting compensated for it. In my current position, I want to develop sales skills so I can interface better with our affiliates. We're selling an idea to them in addition to just performing a service. Regional directors in the sales organization have some skills that I don't have, like contract negotiation. There's a lot of room for growth and movement. I could move from being a regional team leader to being the team leader of a national accounts group team. It's a larger portfolio of accounts, more subscribers, greater revenue.

At one time, if you were a bean counter, you were always a bean counter. Today we have people who moved from financial services into the sales organization, and other people who moved from sales into financial services. There's more room for movement within the organization.

One of the really nice things since reengineering is that my relationships with customers have changed. With the team approach, all the customers in our region know who we are, and we stay in touch on a regular basis. We don't just call because they didn't pay their bill right or owe us money. Sometimes we call just to see how things are going.

We also get out of the office and talk to clients. We try to find out from them how we can provide better services. That's the kind of contact we never had before. It makes my job a lot more fun.

Within the company, I've been able to contribute more and to learn more. I learn from team members and other leaders and share my knowledge and experience. I think there's more respect all around.

Also, management is much more open with us. That's really important. Now you know things almost as soon as they happen. I received a copy of my team's budget in today's interoffice mail with last year's forecast, the year-to-date actuals, to what degree we're over or under. In the old days, it was unheard-of to know the real numbers.

I don't know that I'll stay at Showtime forever. But whatever moves I make, I could never go back to the old kind of organization. I'm really challenged and stimulated by the work.

BOB RANKIN OF GTE

A need to respond more quickly and efficiently prompted GTE Corporation of Florida to reengineer its process for handling customers' requests for repairs and new service. In the field, the company eliminated a number of supervisory positions and divided its service technicians into small teams with responsibility for specific geographic areas, giving them control over dispatching and reporting. Armed with cellular telephones and laptop computers, the technicians manage their own work.

The new process focus has expanded workers' responsibilities and required many changes in their daily lives. Some employees find the changes stressful and difficult to accept, but many others—like Bob Rankin, who repairs and maintains GTE telephone systems in Sarasota—delight in them.

In our zone, there are five technicians in the group. There's one young man who does installation work. The other four are veteran facility maintainers. We're having a very good time under the new system. They've given us the freedom to work on our own. We're doing real well with it.

For me, I've been at GTE for twenty-three years, and I always thought we were overmanaged, controlled, and supervised. When you've got one supervisor for every eight to ten employees, that's way too much.

In the old days, the supervisors used to encourage us to call them at the drop of a hat. "If you have any questions or doubts about what you're doing, give us a call and we'll be glad to jump in our truck and talk to the customer and you about the problem." They treated us like children.

Sometimes they could help, but it usually wasn't necessary. For example, if we had an irate subscriber, we'd call our supervisor who would come out and calm the guy down. The customer responded to his "shirt and tie and company vehicle." Now we don't have the tie, but we can deal with them. We've been working with the public and literally going into their homes day in and day out for many, many years.

We're also developing ongoing relationships with the customers. The fact that you've got four or five people zoned in a certain geographical area means that we get personally familiar with our customers' equipment and problems. We can take care of some things through preventive maintenance along with our daily assigned work.

We also have more interest now in how well things get fixed. That's human nature. Traditionally, you had a large number of guys who didn't have to be accountable for their actions. In other words, they might be tempted to make that quick fix to get something corrected, but not necessarily do it right the first time. Now, when you've got only four or five guys and the customer knows them personally, you know that if you don't fix it correctly the first time it's going to come back to haunt you. There's much more pride in ownership. You have self-esteem and all those sorts of things.

There's much more job satisfaction than there ever was, too. We used to come to work, do our jobs, and go home. Talk about piecemeal assembly-line work! That's basically how most of us felt about our jobs.

Some people think the new freedom and responsibility are more stressful, but not me. I thought the old setup was stressful because they didn't treat us with nearly as much trust and dignity as now. We've assumed a large majority of former management duties and taken responsibility and accountability for our actions.

This is the most intelligent thing this company has done in years. We basically all feel that way. It's fun. It's nice being your own boss and knowing you don't need to make a phone call every time you have a little bit of a challenge. It's not necessary and never was necessary. Any major corporation needs to think about empowering its employees. There's no doubt about it. This change is long overdue.

DIANE GRIFFIN OF AETNA

Aetna Life & Casualty Company may have deserved an award for simpleminded tasks and complicated processes with an approach to applications handling that took an average of twenty-eight days to do twenty-six minutes of work. Each tiny task was performed by a different worker. It didn't take long to perform any of them—entering the application, rating it, or responding to the customer—but the delays in transit were brutal. At every stop, it had to work its way to the top of someone's in-box.

Aetna now has a reengineered "one and done" process: Each application is handled by a single customer account manager. For nearly twelve years, Diane Griffin performed one small, mind-numbing task in Aetna's Tampa, Florida, office. Now she is a customer account manager who handles the whole process herself.

In the old days, each business application that came into our department was handled by many different people. A form processor would process the work in, a rater would calculate the premium, an input operator would put the material into the system. A different department would type it up, and another one would send it out to the customer. Now we've combined the functions. An application comes into the office and goes straight to a customer account manager. We process it, rate it, and input it into the system. Then it is mailed out from this department. The work is now "one and done"—one person gets it, and all the work is done by them.

It's made a big difference in how we work and how we see our work. Now we can see the customers as individual people. It's no longer "us" and "them"; it's helped us realize that, without "them," there would be no "us." It has made a better relationship.

In the beginning, when we were training for the new jobs, there was a lot of overtime and people were unhappy. But the more we saw how the new system speeded up the process, the more we liked it. With most of the busywork gone, we can concentrate more on the customer's needs and on trying to make sure everything is done correctly.

We're also working on teams now. Before, you would get your work and you didn't pay attention to what other people were doing. If you did well, you got a raise at the end of the year. Now there is a bonus for what you do well and also for what your team does. As a team member, everybody wants to get a bonus. So you make sure the team does well and you become more of a team player.

The best thing that has happened is that now the workers feel involved and appreciated. We used to think, "They will never let go of their power and their management environment," but as time goes on, they have given us more and more training and they really are listening to us. We have meetings once a week where we can voice our opinions, and if something is going on in the team that you think you can make better, you are allowed to voice it out and discuss it. For example, we used to be set up in two groups, with one side handling certain agents and the other side handling other agents. But that meant that on some days one person might get more phone calls than another. So we decided as a team that when a call comes in, whoever is available gets it. It distributes the work equally, and we are sharing the load so that one person doesn't get bogged down.

Most of the teams have team leaders who make the final decision on the guidelines and regulations. The leader also makes sure everyone is trained and up to standards, but other than that we are our own managers. The other team members even do the training. Whatever area you feel you are strongest in, you train somebody else in that area.

If there are problems on the team, we work them out. If someone makes a mistake, we don't lash out at them, but we do tell them about it. We learned in our customer service training that it is better to bring a mistake to someone's attention than to let them keep on making the same mistake. And if someone is having a hard time, we pair them up with someone who is good in that area, who can show them how to do it right. You have to be aware that everyone learns at a different pace, but everyone is still learning. The key is your attitude toward everything.

Another thing that we do is have a team meeting every week. We talk about any problems we might see and get to the root of them. It's really just good communications.

It also helps us learn. I know a lot more about underwriting and business, why we do certain things. I've been here twelve years now and hope to be here another twelve years.

The main thing that has happened is that the work is a lot more satisfying because you are focused on customers and wanting to help them. I feel a sense of gratitude.

The company is letting me do the best job that I can do. They have shown us confidence. I feel appreciated and am not just a number anymore.

The recurring themes here are apparent. Deborah Phelps, Bob Rankin, and Diane Griffin have all moved from performing narrow tasks to positions where they perform an entire process and where they are measured not by the number of things they do but by the caliber of their results. Their new jobs are more complex, but they also have more control over how they organize their work and what they do all day. Their new positions not only entail more responsibility and autonomy, but also involve change, learning, and intensity. They must take risks to get rewards. And most importantly, no one is looking over their shoulders to check on each decision and action. Our business lexicon needs a new word to describe people like these working as they now do.

CHAPTER 3

FROM WORKER TO PROFESSIONAL

EARLY POLITICAL economists from Adam Smith to Karl Marx recognized that production drives psychology, that people's mentalities are shaped by how they do their work. On the eve of the twenty-first century, this insight remains important: As the workplace changes, jobs change and, as a result, the people working in those jobs will change as well.

During the Industrial Revolution, craftsmen and laborers flocked from workshops and farms to join the burgeoning army of factory workers. In doing so, they swapped the risk and uncertainty of their former lives for a degree of certainty offered by wage labor. But at the same time they traded autonomy for a life of dependence on their employers. Today, at the end of the Industrial Revolution, the nature of work is changing again, and this trade-off is being recalibrated. By focusing on customers and processes, process centering is eliminating both the traditional industrial job and with it the very concept of the industrial worker. In its place is arising the large, process-centered job that must be filled by a new type of "professional" worker. This new professional recaptures the autonomy of the pre-industrial artisan, but in a market-focused entrepreneurial environment. This new bargain is not better or worse than the old one, but it is different and its implications are far-reaching.

To understand the nature of the transition from worker to professional, and to understand why it is inevitable, we need an understanding of what happens to processes when they begin to receive the attention that they deserve. When processes come to the fore in an organization's consciousness, their shortcomings become apparent and are addressed. To appreciate these short-comings, we need to introduce some terminology to describe the component activities of any process.

All work activities can be classified into three types:

- Value-adding work, or work for which the customer is willing to pay
- Non-value-adding work, which creates no value for the customer but is required in order to get the value-adding work done
- Waste, or work that neither adds nor enables value

Value-adding work is easy to identify. It consists of all of the activities that create the goods and services that customers want. If a customer wants an order filled, value-adding activities include inventory allocation, picking, packing, route planning, and shipping. Value-adding work can rarely be eliminated from a process, although it can be improved.

Waste work is pointless work whose absence would, by definition, not be noticed by the customer. Producing reports that no one reads, doing work erroneously so that it needs to be redone, redundant checking activities—these are all waste work. Waste work needs to be eliminated root and branch.

Most companies deserve pretty good marks for how they deal with these two categories of work. After fifty years of automation, mechanization, industrial engineering, and time-and-motion studies, most companies perform productive work quite efficiently. Similarly, after a decade or more of quality improvement efforts, they have managed to identify and eliminate much of the waste work. However, the same cannot yet be said of non-value-adding work.

Non-value-adding work is the glue that binds together the value-adding work in conventional processes. It is all the administrative overhead—the reporting, checking, supervising, controlling, reviewing, and liaising. It is work that is needed to make conventional processes function, but it is also the source of errors, delay, inflexibility, and rigidity. It adds expense and complexity to processes, and makes them error-prone and hard to understand or change.

Over the years, non-value-adding work in large organizations has expanded to the point where it often dominates and exceeds the value-adding work. It is not at all uncommon to find less than 10 percent of the activities in a process to be value-adding, with the rest mostly non-value-adding overhead. But this baggage cannot simply be discarded. If you were to take the non-value-adding work out of a traditional process, the process would collapse. Instead, it is necessary to *design* the non-value-adding work out by reorganizing the value-adding tasks into a new and more efficient process. Once processes become the center of organizational attention, the non-value-adding overhead that burdens them becomes apparent, and redesign efforts are undertaken to rid the processes of it. (Often, but not always, these efforts are labeled "reengineering.")

The consequences of redesigning processes to reduce non-value-adding work are many and significant. The first of these is that jobs become bigger and more complex. One way to appreciate this fact is through the use of an eggshell metaphor. The Industrial Age broke processes into series of small tasks. Think of these as the myriad fragments of an eggshell. To reassemble these fragments into an entire shell requires an enormous amount of glue—and when completed, the reassembled structure will be fragile, unstable, and ugly. Each ragged seam is a potential trouble spot. Moreover, since glue is more expensive than eggshell, the reconstructed shell will be quite expensive. Similarly, when work is broken into small and simple tasks, one needs complex processes full of non-value-adding glue—reviews, managerial audits, checks, approvals, etc.—to put them back together. Those myriad interactions lead to departmental as well as personal miscommunications, misunderstandings, squabbles, reconciliations, telephone calls— headaches too numerous to list. Furthermore, they give rise to handoffs, interstices, and dark corners where errors lurk and overhead costs breed.

The only way to avoid using so much glue is to start with bigger fragments—in other words, bigger jobs. That is the heart of process centering. A process focus changes the boundaries of traditional jobs, expanding their scope and breadth, so that less non-value-adding effort is required to put them together.

The most common way of doing this is simply to have jobs encompass a larger number of value-adding tasks. At GTE, for example, responding to a customer's report of an outage involves three value-adding tasks: getting the information from the customer, checking GTE's own equipment and lines, and, if necessary, dispatching a repair person. Formerly performed by three specialists, all three tasks are now performed by one person—a customer care advocate. When three people are involved, there is a need for coordination, communication, and checking; not so when one person is involved.

Even when one person cannot perform an entire process, it is still possible to have every person who is involved in the process understand it in its entirety and focus on its outcome. When people appreciate the larger context of their work they do not work at cross purposes with others engaged in the same process. When everyone has a common measure there is no need for reconciling inconsistent activities. When people are all on the same side their energy goes into avoiding errors instead of allocating blame for them. In short, process centering eliminates the need for non-value-adding work by creating bigger jobs for those who perform the value-adding work.

The starting point of the Industrial Age organization—simple jobs for simple people—inevitably led to complex, and consequently poorly performing, processes. In the modern age, the need is to have simple and lean processes. This means that jobs must be more complex. We replace simple jobs and complex processes with simple processes and complex jobs.

Let's look more closely at the "big jobs" that process centering creates, like the GTE customer care advocate (CCA). No longer limited to a single task, the CCA is now responsible for the full range of work required to resolve a customer's problem. Focused on the outcome rather than on any single activity, the CCA's goal is not merely the proper performance of a task or a combination of tasks but the achievement of a desired result. If that result isn't accomplished, a CCA can't say, "I did my job and it's not my fault that things didn't work well."

GTE must still take customer information and perform testing and dispatching. The difference is that now one person does all these things with a single goal in mind: solving the customer's problem. To this end the CCA must be proficient in several distinct kinds of activities and have knowledge of multiple disciplines. He or she must know how to talk to customers and to use sophisticated software programs. The CCA must grasp the essentials of diagnosing faulty telephone lines and have a feeling for the art as well as the science of dispatching. It is essential for the CCA to be able to judge the priority to assign to particular customers, especially in crunch times such as weather-caused emergencies. The CCA's "people" skills must be sufficiently developed to sense what kind of service representative to send to a particular customer or situation. A CCA is also trained in GTE's products and services so as to recommend solutions to customer problems that the CCA perceives. This is indeed a "big" job.

It's important to realize that the CCA is not just a quick-change artist, switching a customer service representative's hat for a line-testing helmet and then for a dispatch bonnet. The CCA needs to maintain a holistic perspective in order to ensure that all these tasks fit together. He or she must get enough information in the first phase to do the work of the second phase and to choose the right service representative should the third phase prove necessary. Everything is interrelated. In short, the CCA's job is both big (because it entails many different activities) and complex (since all these activities are mutually dependent).

This phenomenon is not unique to the GTE customer care advocate. It is intrinsic to all process-centered jobs. At Cleveland-based Progressive Insurance, claims adjusters handle almost the entire process of responding to policyholders' claims after car accidents. They check to see that policies are indeed in force, they schedule their own appointments, they file claims after inspection of damaged cars, and they decide on the spot how best to handle the claim. At Monsanto Chemical, production workers involved in the manufacture of polymer fibers are no longer focused on single steps in the process: making the polymer, spinning it into a fiber, steaming it to produce the right kind of threads, or cutting them to the proper lengths. As manufacturing process performers, they appreciate the entire process and are focused on the end product. They visit customers in order to learn how their products are used and what their customers require. They are concerned with, and responsible for, a great variety of variables: fiber strength, operating temperatures, and color. Both individually and collectively they make decisions about the operation of the process and how it can be improved. At Federal-Mogul, a distributor and manufacturer of auto parts, engineers working on the process of developing samples of new products for customer evaluation are no longer exclusively confined to the design activity. They work with customers and sales representatives to define the customer's needs, they interact with tooling and manufacturing specialists to assure that the sample can and will be made on time, and they share with all other performers of the process the responsibility to assure that the process is operating well.

The "little" person doing a little task is going the way of the rotary-dial telephone. People working in high-performance processes do many tasks and must attend to how they fit together and how they lead to meeting the customer's needs. To do this, they must be able to see the big picture. They must see how all the pieces of their process—and other processes— fit together to create value for the customer. This is not just an abstract desire, it is an absolute requirement. Traditionally, an engineer needed only to be an engineer, a sales rep only a sales rep, a production worker that and nothing else. The operating assumption was that if everyone took care of his or her piece, the result would take care of itself. We have learned that this is dangerously false and that in reality no one was taking care of the end result. In the process-centered company, everyone must. The engineer working on product development must still be an engineer, but, more than that, he or she must also understand marketing, production, customer service, and everything else associated with developing a product—and how they dovetail.

The elimination of non-value-adding work also has consequences for how people spend their time and direct their energy. Consider again an engineer. Most engineering graduates hired by traditional companies are excited about the prospect of putting their new skills to work. But they soon discover that real engineering is only a small part of what they actually do in their jobs. They spend much of their days filling out forms, preparing budgets, attending meetings with people from other departments, and responding to other people's reviews of their work. All these activities take place under multiple levels of supervision—and to satisfy internal, not customer, imperatives. In other words, engineers must perform a wide range of non-value-adding activities that have little relevance to what they had believed to be the heart of their profession. Frustration, boredom, and numbness result, usually in that order—with predictable results for organizational performance.

The shift to a process-centered orientation changes all this. Most non-value-adding work lurks at boundaries, both vertical and horizontal, and a process focus dissolves those boundaries. When they are gone, the preponderance of busywork goes with them.

The Progressive adjuster doesn't waste time bargaining with supervisors, coordinating with dispatchers, or seeking approvals from management. The adjuster spends his or her time *adjusting*. The Monsanto production workers no longer hang around waiting for the foreman's directions or approval. Operating as a team, they just go and get the work done. An engineer in a process-centered organization does engineering work, not administrative work. The virtual absence of non-value-adding work means that people doing real work don't have to waste time performing non-value-adding work. They don't have to be distracted by it, and they don't even have to deal with other people who are doing it. They can concentrate on the *real* work.

This change goes far beyond savings in time: It transforms attitudes. In traditional organizations, many idealistic, ambitious young people soon come to describe their jobs as routine and boring. But process-centered environments allow workers to concentrate on substantive work that capitalizes on their imagination and resourcefulness. People are too important, too valuable, and too capable of doing important work to waste on routine and repetition.

The new operating principle is, "If I can tell you precisely what to do, then I don't need you to do it. I can tell a machine to do it, and the machine is cheaper and doesn't need vacations." The only work left for humans to do is work that truly requires human capabilities.

While process centering frees people from administrative hassles and liberates them from drone work, it also places new demands on them. Often, a rational and efficient process will feel like a marathon relay. Dramatically increasing the ratio of real work to busywork may be a boon to the spirit, but it can also be a great drain on the body. Spending most of the day in substantive pursuits burns up enormous amounts of energy and relentlessly wears down one's nerves. The engineer who finds meetings with finance and marketing to be tedious may also be secretly grateful for the opportunity they provide to relax a bit. When the well-designed process eliminates that bit of slack time—when, for instance, needed communications between engineers, marketing experts, and financial people are suddenly transformed into totally efficient electronic interactions—meetings become intense problem-solving sessions rather than stupefying time killers. The engineer may find himself working at full steam all day, all week, all year. This is a fine challenge for many twenty-four-year-olds. Many forty-four-year-olds will find it exhausting.

Process-centered measurements reinforce this sense of urgency and intensity. Because such measurements look at results rather than activities, they offer a cold and indisputable gauge of performance. In a traditional environment it is essentially impossible to determine the exact effect of anyone's individual work on the ultimate result, so managers fall back on surrogate measures that concentrate on task productivity.

Thus in the old days GTE's customer service representatives were assessed by how many calls they handled per hour; it was assumed that this would correlate with customer satisfaction. But when you think about it, this is not a very plausible assumption. A service rep could become adept at merely saying, "Hello. I don't know. Good-bye." This would drive up official performance measures but not do much for customers. And when customer satisfaction would ultimately prove to be low, service reps could duck responsibility, claiming they had done their jobs. By contrast, a CCA is evaluated on process outcome, namely customer satisfaction. The specific measurements that GTE uses for this are the time required to resolve problems and the percentage of resolutions achieved on the customer's first call (which now exceeds 33 percent).

A CCA cannot hide from or argue with these figures. It doesn't matter how hard a CCA works or how many calls he or she fields: It only matters how well the process performs.

This measurement shift puts more pressure on people. In a fragmented organization, weak individual performance often doesn't matter much and can even go unnoticed amid the ineffectual performance of the system as a whole. In a process-centered environment, each team member is personally on the line for the result. Subpar or half-hearted contributions by anyone will show up in the results of the process. Everyone must always perform, as one CEO has put it, "at threshold levels, maximum levels, target levels." There is no place to hide or any place to goof off.

Eliminating essentially empty work that adds no value also increases the pressure to do more real work. Gresham's Law in economics states that "bad money drives out good": People will spend worthless currency and keep it in circulation while they hoard money that has intrinsic value. A corresponding business axiom is that "the immediate drives out the important." How often have you told your boss—or yourself—that the budget review, the committee report, or an urgent personnel matter poached the time you'd scheduled for your creative work? But when most of the supplementary stuff has vanished, you're on the line for your real work.

Non-value-adding work may have been soul-destroying, but at least it provided excuses for not performing real work. No longer. The pressure is intense, the spotlight is on, and neither one relents.

Further, it is no longer possible for workers to shirk responsibility by saying that the "boss" is the one accountable for results. What boss? There is no place for the conventional supervisor in the process-centered organization. "Supervision" is only a meaningful word when it is preceded by "task."

Narrow and simple tasks can be overseen by a supervisor, who bears the ultimate responsibility for their performance. But no outsider or overseer can "supervise" an individual or a team performing the wide range of tasks that constitute a process. In a process-centered organization, there are no convenient organizational handoffs at which a supervisor can be stationed to monitor the results of tasks and inspect intermediate work products. Work is a continuum, not a series of discrete pieces, and nothing can be said to be done until the whole is done. The "handoffs" are now informal or even more importantly internal—inside people's heads. There is no place or role for the traditional supervisor, and with the supervisor's disappearance goes the last line of excuses for the frontline worker. The supervisor isn't in charge and on the line—the worker is.

Autonomy and responsibility are integral to process-centered jobs. Workers who merely work and managers who only manage condemn companies to be dysfunctional organizations full of managers who don't do real work and workers who don't have enough responsibility or knowledge to get the work done right. Such organizations are simply too expensive, wasteful, and fraught with potential for conflict and error to survive. They require too many layers of non-value-adding overhead, and they are doomed to inflexibility because they deprive workers of the authority and the perspective to use their own initiative.

In a process-centered organization, self-managed workers are responsible for both performing work and assuring that it is well-done. There is no longer a great divide between "doing" and "managing." Management is no longer an esoteric and inaccessible skill reserved for a remote and privileged elite. It becomes part of *everyone's* job.

Even in a fast-food operation like Taco Bell, frontline workers are assuming greater management roles or, more precisely, what used to be considered management roles. They pay bills, handle emergencies, and defuse customer complaints on the spot. Taco Bell's ultimate goal, to have teams so well-trained and customer-responsive that they require no supervision, may be utopian, but not by much. One shift worker at a Taco Bell restaurant says that he and his co-workers already feel "like we're running our own business. And who doesn't want to run his own business?"

Let us review the characteristics of jobs in a process-centered environment. In order for the process to be free of non-value-adding work, the jobs will be big and complex, covering a range of tasks and demanding that the job holder understand the big picture: business goals, customer needs, process structure. As non-value-adding work is eliminated, jobs become more substantive and consequently more difficult, more challenging, and more intense. Along with these characteristics come responsibility for results, personal autonomy, and the authority to make decisions. In short, process-centered jobs have virtually nothing in common with traditional industrial era jobs, whether blue, pink, or white collar. They do have a great deal in common with the kinds of jobs normally held by professionals. The inevitable consequence of process centering an organization is professionalizing its work.

Conventionally, the term professional has been used to refer to physicians, attorneys, architects, accountants, and the like. While these conventional professionals all have advanced academic training, that is not their defining characteristic. A professional is someone who is responsible for achieving a result rather than performing a task. You don't go to a doctor to have your throat examined, your blood pressure taken, or your heart checked. You go to the doctor to get well. The physician's focus must not be on activity, but on outcome. The goal of a good physician is not taking many pulses and looking at many throats, but curing many patients. The attorney's client is not interested in the quantity or even the quality of the briefs and arguments that the attorney makes. The client only cares whether or not the case is won. An architect is someone who creates a design for a building, not someone who does renderings or computes stresses. The tasks get done, but it is the outcome—produced by a process—that truly defines the work of the professional.

In this sense, process performers like the GTE customer care advocate, the Progressive claims adjuster, and the Monsanto production worker are also professionals. They may not have advanced degrees—although they are likely to have significant training and education, which we will discuss later—but they are as professional as any physician.

Three words characterize the worldview of a professional: customer, result, process. The professional sees himself or herself as responsible to the *customer;* the mission is to solve a problem for the customer, to create the value that the customer requires. If that value is not created, if that problem is not solved, the professional has not done his or her job. It is only by producing the *result* that the customer requires—by performing the entire *process* that yields that result—that the professional discharges his or her responsibility. In contrast, a worker is focused on three other words: boss, activity, task. The worker's ultimate goal is to please the boss, since it is in the boss's hands that the worker's income and future lie. So the worker seeks to keep busy, to maintain a high activity level performing the task that the boss has assigned. Sales reps are eager to secure orders, customer service people listen to complaints, file clerks file, but no one has any concern for the totality of the work.

A professional is a cross between a worker and a manager, responsible both for performing work and for assuring its successful completion. A professional will never say, "It's not my job," or sing Johnny Paycheck's song "Take This Job and Shove It," or assert that life begins at 5:00 P.M. Perhaps the best definition of a professional is "someone who does what it takes." In contrast, a traditional worker is "someone who does what he or she is told." Whether working alone or as a member of a team, the professional's mission is to achieve an objective. He or she may be given guidelines, tools, and advice about recommended practices, but the ultimate goal is to obtain the needed result, not to perform tasks or follow instructions.

This distinction between worker and professional replaces such outmoded ones as blue collar/white collar, hourly/salaried, production workers/knowledge workers. All people today must work with their heads, not just with their hands. Production work does not mean mindless drone work. The people on the factory floor today at Hill's Pet Nutrition or Monsanto Chemical have little in common with a factory hand at Henry Ford's old River Rouge plant. The people at Monsanto and Hill's are professionals.

The difference between a worker and a professional is not merely a terminological one. Their work is different, their behavior is different, and what is required of them is entirely different. Workers inhabit precisely defined jobs and operate under close supervision, while professionals can be constrained by neither. A professional who is focused on customers and outcomes cannot be burdened with many rules; the professional's goal is not to follow rules, but to get the job done. A worker is a kind of organic robot, operated by a manager via remote control. A professional is an independent human being. Once provided with knowledge and a clear understanding of the goal, professionals can be expected to get there on their own. At Nordstrom's, sales personnel working the department store floor are treated as professionals and expected to follow one basic rule: Use your best judgment in all situations. At Nordstrom's, sales personnel are not automatons, preprogrammed to carry out tightly specified orders. In a world of constant change, no possible set of orders, no library of guidelines, could be comprehensive enough to cover every circumstance. When the goal keeps shifting and the road to reach it requires improvisation, the intelligence and autonomy of the professional must supplant the obedience and predictability of the worker.

Describing how she sees her place in the scheme of things, a woman at the Bank of Bermuda told me her motto, which I offer as the reigning ethic of the process-centered environment. "If it is to be," she said, "it's up to me." The buck stops at everyone's desk. Indeed, it never gets passed in the first place.

In a traditional organization, only those workers who must directly interact with customers ever encounter them. But all professionals, no matter what their specific role, must understand customers so that they know how their own work contributes to meeting customer needs. Commerce Clearing House (CCH) is a leading publisher of tax and business law information based in Riverwoods, Illinois. In the old days, editors at CCH could work for decades without ever talking to a living, breathing customer. Now every editor and every other professional learns how the company's products are actually used by spending on-site time with customers. Workers at Monsanto's plant in Decatur, Alabama, who make acrylic fibers for upholstery, now visit customers to see how their products are used. This customer awareness reinforces the self-image that people are producers of products and services rather than mere jobholders. Peter Clark, the plant manager of Monsanto's Decatur plant, says that people who were formerly programmed to do a task now see themselves as making products—and are determined to make them well because they know what happens to these products when they leave the factory. His people sometimes even argue with him over decisions that they think may cause problems for customers. Such expressions of concern would never have been heard from task-oriented workers.

This concern for the product and the customer's response to it affects even those who discharge what were once considered "staff" responsibilities. Bruce Carswell, the recently retired senior vice president for human resources at GTE, remembers that ten years ago human relations people like himself were concerned only with their own specialized activities. Now he says he couldn't pursue his line of work without spending 70 percent of his time in the field. He feels he must know both the businesses he's trying to help and their customers as well as he knows his own discipline. Otherwise, "I'd be sitting here thinking great thoughts that nobody needs."

To be a professional a person needs education as well as training. The presumption that workers do only simple jobs allows organizations to view them as empty vessels into which the instructions for task performance can be poured. A professional, by contrast, doesn't work according to explicit instructions. Directed toward a goal and provided with significant latitude, the professional must be a problem-solver—able to cope with unanticipated and unusual situations without running to management for guidance. This requires a reservoir of knowledge, a grounding in the discipline that underlies the job as well as an appreciation for how this knowledge can be applied to different situations.

The MIT scholar Donald Schon calls another professional requirement "reflection." He argues that an effective professional not only performs work, but also *reflects* on it. A true professional is engaged in an ongoing inquiry, an endless quest for insight into and understanding of his or her practice. The professional examines what is effective and what is not, tries to identify successful and unsuccessful techniques, and fashions theories to be applied in the future. The professional is a constant learner, not only in the classroom but in the field. The worker is trained; the professional learns.

True professionalism also overwhelms petty differences and distinctions inside an organization. When we are all focused on customers and results, the distinction between my work and your work becomes insignificant. Real professionals naturally take to a team environment because their overriding concern is getting the job done. This does not mean that ego and specialized expertise wither away in a process-centered organization. What does happen, however, is that competitive energy is redirected from inside the organization to outside. Instead of individual workers vying for supervisory attention and approval, professionals work together to achieve a result for which they will all receive credit. No matter how strong the personalities involved, a shared objective—a common focus on an outcome desired by all members of a team—inevitably promotes cooperation.

Professionals have a connection with the results of their efforts. One of the most profound, albeit unintended, consequences of the Industrial Age was the disconnection of workers from products and the customers who benefited from their work. Anomie is the sociologist's term to describe the rootlessness, alienation, disconnection, and isolation that is endemic to the Industrial Age. The origins of this may be traced to the transition from artisan and peasant to factory worker in the early nineteenth century. On their farms and in their cottages, however wretched the conditions, people saw the outcome and knew the purpose of their labor, and it helped give them a sense of identity. They knew the full cycle of tasks and their own relationship to the result.

Performing an isolated task cannot provide the gratification that comes from closure and a sense of contribution. When the fruit of one's labor is visible, the laborer feels intimately connected to it. Paint a wall and you step back to look, not only to check for missed patches but also to enjoy the sense of accomplishment that comes from the result—not from mixing the paint or cleaning the brushes. Process-oriented work affords the satisfaction of creating a product or serving a customer. Professional, process-oriented jobs are whole jobs.

When I am asked what I do for a living, I sometimes (half-facetiously) reply, "I'm reversing the Industrial Revolution." The Industrial Revolution decomposed processes into tasks; process centering puts them back together. This reversion from task to process restores to work some of the meaning it had in the pre-modern era. It is only relatively recently in human history that work became thought of as a purely commercial transaction in which time and labor were sold to an employer in exchange for money. Before that, your work was your identity and your calling as well as your daily bread. Despite the changes of the Industrial Revolution, this has continued for a lucky or chosen or determined few. Ask physicians or attorneys what they do. Their answer defines who they are. A doctor will say, "I am a physician," not "I give medical examinations" or "I treat diabetes." You've asked about activity, you're answered in terms of identity—because professionals live their work. Professional work is not an activity performed a certain number of hours a day, but one's persona, one's essence.

The need for new vocabulary does not end with the use of

performer and professional instead of worker. The term "job" needs replacement as well. Workers have jobs; professionals have careers. A job is predefined, a hole into which a suitable peg will be made to fit. A career is built around an individual. As the peg grows and changes shape, the hole is redrilled. A job belongs to the company. "My job" is an oxymoron, since the company can eliminate or take away the job at any time. My career, however, is indeed mine. I may choose to spend much or all of it at a single company, but my career exists independently of that company. And the responsibility for managing my career is mine.

Home Depot, the spectacularly successful retailer of hardware and home improvement materials, tells its people flat out that while other retailers offer jobs, Home Depot offers careers. The people who work at Home Depot are carpenters and plumbers who don't so much sell building supplies as help customers solve their home improvement problems. Such people have real autonomy, are paid more than sales clerks, and are key to Home Depot's success.

A career is not merely a series of jobs. It is better described in terms of personal learning and development. Professionals do not look to "advance"; their goal is to become better professionals and thereby to reap the rewards of better performance. This has long been true of conventional professions, and it is true of the new professionals as well. For instance, Bob Roberts, an Aetna vice president, has observed that Aetna's customer account managers—the people who process an insurance application from start to finish—model their career expectations on those of physicians. Physicians expect to do better for themselves by learning more and doing better for their patients.

Aetna's customer account managers are following the same pattern. Over time they learn to handle more accounts and accounts of greater sophistication. The resulting increase in business produces more income for Aetna and for them. Their income gain comes from growth in their professional abilities, not from longevity or mounting another rung in a hierarchical ladder. This personal growth in knowledge, capability, and mastery provides not only increased income but increased stature. The most highly respected people in a profession are not those with the greatest authority but those with the greatest knowledge. It is the best attorney, the best architect, the best physician whom others admire and seek to emulate, not the ones who have the most people working for them. A professional career does not concentrate on position and power but on knowledge, capability, and influence.

A process-centered worker can best be described as a self-employed professional, a hybrid of a professional and an entrepreneur. Performing a process is in very many ways a great deal like running one's own business. A process, just like a business, has customers and measures of overall performance. A successful entrepreneur is, above all, intensely focused on his customers. He defines his business not in terms of a particular set of products and services but in terms of meeting customer needs. The entrepreneur dispenses with bureaucracy and formality in order to deliver customer value. The focus is on getting the right things done. People working in an entrepreneurial context cannot afford to worry about organizational appurtenances and boundaries. While each may have a specific primary responsibility, they all have an appreciation for the business as a whole and a visceral recognition of how their performance and their future are linked with those of the company as a whole. All of these themes also appear in the process environment. Everyone working there is focused on the customer, puts first the needs of the process as a whole, and will do what it takes to get the job done.

The transition from worker to professional is a sea change in the nature of work, and it entails many changes—from empowerment gained to security lost, from alienation overcome to an encounter with the danger of burn-out, satisfaction bought at the price of high anxiety. These changes are inevitable and all flow from the renaissance of process and the consequent transformation of work. Process centering creates professionals.

CHAPTER 4

YES, BUT WHAT DOES IT MEAN FOR ME?

THERE IS an enormous gap between intellectually understanding an idea and really appreciating what it means. The first is conceptual, the second is personal and experiential. While it is not particularly difficult to comprehend the abstract notion of the task worker giving way to the process professional, it is quite something else for an individual to come to terms with how this transition affects his or her own life. As we have seen, as organizations focus themselves on processes, job requirements, measurements, and rewards all change. The result is an entirely new world of work. For most people, it is more satisfying and rewarding, but it is assuredly very different.

As people try to envision what it would be like to live in such an environment, they generally focus on four questions:

- Will I succeed in this new world of work?
- How—and how much—will I be paid?
- What title will I have?
- What sort of future can I expect?

It's been said that every great idea eventually degenerates into hard work. Similarly, every great concept ultimately succeeds or fails in the arena of self-interest. It is with such personal questions, rather than abstract ones, that most people are intensely concerned. Let's consider them in order.

Will I succeed in this new world of work?

It seems evident that in a world of professional work, the key to personal success is to be a professional. This does not mean that everyone needs to have postgraduate training. It does mean, however, that we will have to transform ourselves into the kinds of people who are capable of filling professional roles. Some of the professions required in process-centered organizations have well-established identities: sales, marketing, engineering, finance, and the like. But customer service representatives, production personnel, and all sorts of other workers will also have to become professionals in their own ways. The service representative must begin thinking—and operating—as a professional problem solver, not just as someone prepared to answer a predictable set of customer inquiries. Similarly, the production worker must become an operations professional, knowledgeable about the manufacturing process and what's necessary to make it work. Everyone must have a professional mind-set.

Success in any profession has three prerequisites: knowledge, perspective, and attitude. No professional can succeed without a solid grounding in the basic discipline that he or she must apply at work. Obviously, every individual must make a strong personal commitment to learning the particular skills that his or her job requires. But the knowledge of a professional goes far beyond basic skills. A professional must know the concepts of the field, the principles and ideas that have far longer lifetimes than constantly changing facts and techniques. Professionals must also be committed to ongoing learning—many professions in fact demand it as a condition of accreditation. We all know that ten years from now surgeons will be performing operations and accountants will be applying tax laws that no one had heard of in 1996. Similarly, production personnel will be using new techniques and customer service reps will be dealing with new problems. If they don't keep themselves up to date, they will find themselves former production personnel and service reps.

Becoming a professional demands more than just assimilating and maintaining a body of knowledge. It also means having a special perspective, a characteristic style of thinking. Professionals do not simply follow rote algorithms. As we saw in chapter 3, routine activities are becoming an ever smaller component of modern jobs. Routine work can be eliminated, automated, or performed by customers. The heart of adding value comes from applying knowledge and creativity to novel situations. Such problem solving is accomplished by applying a body of knowledge with a particular mode of analysis and synthesis. True professional education teaches such modes of analysis and problem solving. Law schools pride themselves on teaching legal thinking as much as the law; doctors need to know diagnostic technique as much as they do anatomy and physiology. In short, to succeed as a professional you must know how to think. This is not a simple challenge. In traditional organizations, thinking has not been a requisite for many jobs, or even a skill that was much prized. Therefore, most people are quite unprepared to do jobs that require them to think and most companies don't know how to prepare them for these jobs. Such preparation involves education rather than training. Conventional organizations excel at training, at programming workers in the particular tasks they will be called on to perform. Companies will now have to develop the ability to educate, to teach incipient professionals thinking and problem solving. This is not a small undertaking, for either the company or the employee. There is nothing harder to teach or to do than thinking. But people who learn it will never go out of fashion.

Being a professional also means having the proper temperament or attitude. A physician who does not care about his patients, who is not intensely dedicated to doing whatever needs to be done to cure a disease, is not a good physician, no matter how knowledgeable of medicine or skilled at diagnosis.

Fundamentally, all professionals require the same set of attitudes, regardless of their field. The first of these is self-motivation and discipline. A professional may be paid by an organization but is ultimately answerable to his or her profession and the demands of his or her conscience. Professionals do the work correctly not because someone is watching but because it matters to them. A second required attitude is sincerity and enthusiasm; professionals value their work and believe in its importance. The true professional is not merely pursuing a livelihood, but is following a higher calling. Cynicism is not a trait we value in professionals to whom we entrust ourselves. The professional is also tenacious, committed to doing whatever is necessary to get the required result. Such personal attributes, which define an individual's character, are just as important as intelligence and education in qualifying someone to be a professional. FDR was without question the most effective American president of the twentieth century, yet he was (probably accurately) described by Oliver Wendell Holmes as having a second-class mind but a first-class temperament. Intensity, seriousness of purpose, sincerity, self-reliance: These may be classical virtues, but they are also critical requirements for our new, decidedly nonclassical context.

How—and how much—will I be paid?

This is the question that is closest to most people's hearts, and it is also the one with the most frightening answer: as much as you're worth. In a process-centered environment, you are paid for the results that you produce. This may not sound like such a radical notion until you stop to think about how most workers have traditionally been paid.

In traditional pay systems, people are paid for seniority, for showing up, for following rules, for being pleasant to the boss, or perhaps even for performing and completing assigned tasks. But they aren't paid for producing *results*, which is ultimately the only thing that really matters.

A relatively self-evident principle of compensation states that an organization should reward people in a way that encourages the kinds of behavior that the organization desires. Its vulgar restatement is that you get what you pay for. Traditionally, organizations have paid for plodding, unthinking work and inflexible adherence to rules. Unsurprisingly, that is what they have gotten.

The compensation system of a process-centered organization that focuses on reinforcing desired behavior will pay for *results*. If the process is order fulfillment, it will pay for orders filled accurately, on time, and inexpensively. If the goal is product development, then people will be paid for rapidly developing products that customers want. And in customer service, the company will reward speedy resolution of customer problems.

This concept of paying for results is neither revolutionary nor unprecedented. In many ways this is how entrepreneurs have always been paid. When the business prospers, so do they; but if the business does not perform, there is no magical source for their personal income. Similarly, all professionals get paid for results. If the patients don't get well or the clients keep losing their cases, pretty soon the professional has no income. This approach is also the norm in sales. It doesn't matter if a sales rep visits a hundred customers or conducts a thousand product demonstrations or follows the sales manual meticulously—it only matters if he or she actually makes the sale. The salesperson knows a simple fact that people in thousands of other lines of work have yet to learn: The money that each of us takes home each month does not come from the CEO, the stockholders, or from anyone's supervisor. It comes from customers, and only in exchange for, as the saying goes, delivering the goods.

In fragmented organizations, it is virtually impossible to determine how much impact an individual's work has on process results. The process is invisible, and so measurement and compensation are based on surrogates: time worked, opinion of the supervisor, task productivity, and the like. But when process comes to the fore, everyone's work is directly related to the output of the process. It becomes feasible to measure and reward people on what really counts: outcomes.

This no-nonsense approach of pay-for-results may sound harsh, and it does take away the buffer against the ups and downs of real business that large organizations have long provided. But, because it is more objective, it is really much more fair than old compensation systems. No longer will your take-home pay depend on your supervisor's subjective appraisal of your performance. Now your pay will depend first, on the results you and your teammates deliver, which are quite unambiguous; second, on the performance of the entire organization, which is equally unambiguous; and, third, on your contribution to the team's results as assessed by the rest of your team. This latter factor includes some possible subjectivity, but less than might be expected. It is in your teammates' self-interest to judge you fairly, as they expect you will judge them, and individual biases are likely to be washed out by majority opinion.

Such an objective approach to compensation goes a long way toward eliminating some of the nastier aspects of traditional organizations. It is fundamentally degrading when one person's compensation depends on another's *opinion*. In a process-centered organization, you don't have to thank your boss for what he or she has paid you because, in fact, the boss has not *paid* you your money. You have *earned* it, which is an altogether different idea.

There is no universal formula for process-centered compensation. Each organization will have to develop its own pay system, and there will be a great many variations on the theme. However, the basic principle is clear: You will be paid for what you produce, not for who you are. Who you are—in terms of professionalism, skills, and attitudes—will affect what you accomplish, but it will not be what directly determines your income.

Results-based compensation means that part of your paycheck will be "variable" or "at risk." In theory, *all* of your pay should be performance-based. In the short term, however, the amount is more likely to be 20 to 40 percent. A level of at least 20 percent is necessary to influence behavior in a major way, and it will be difficult to go beyond 40 to 50 percent any time soon. To go further in the short term would represent too large a disruption to most people's financial lives. As it is, there will be some serious adjustments to be made. For example, putting down one's "income" on a mortgage application form will not be so straightforward since a major portion of your income won't be guaranteed. "Salaried" people will have to answer such questions as the self-employed have always done—by providing a five-year income history rather than a guaranteed figure for next year.

The inevitable uncertainty and anxiety associated with such a pay system is in part softened by another answer we can give to the question, "How—and how much—will I be paid?" It is "quite a lot, if you perform well." Process-centered organizations create more customer value with lower costs than do traditional organizations. There is more income, therefore, to be shared with those who create that value. Nor can process-centered organizations afford to underpay their people, because the performance of processes depends not only on their designs but on the caliber of the people performing them. Companies will have a real incentive to pay people what they are worth so that they can attract and hold the people they need. This will bring a welcome end to the trend of the last several decades, which has seen a decline in the incomes of American workers. Conventional workers are fungible commodities. Anyone anywhere can learn to do a simple task, and when the people in developing countries around the world do so, the consequences are inevitable: jobs going abroad and American workers experiencing declining wage rates. Professionals, however, are not so readily replaced. The investment that individuals (and their employers) make in professional education represents an asset that is not easily overcome.

These increased income levels are not simply handed out; they must be earned. The emerging pattern in process-centered compensation systems is that people's base pay will often be lower than their salaries had previously been, but results-based incentives provide the potential for a significant increase in income. In other words, you have to produce just to stay even, but if you do well, you can do very well indeed.

It is interesting to note that in conventional organizations, only senior managers are paid on results. It is only at the top of the organization that all the bits of work come together and that results (typically in the form of a profit and loss statement) can be assessed. But in a process-centered organization, results (in the form of measured process outcomes) can be ascertained throughout the organization, so everyone can be paid as only senior managers used to be.

This is just one of the ways in which process centering democratizes the traditional organization. A conventional organization is a class-based society with a proletariat of frontline workers, a bourgeoisie of middle managers, and an aristocracy of senior executives. It is not just the perquisites, the rides on the corporate plane, and the stock options that are reserved for the upper classes. They are actually seen as a different class of humanity. They get to see the big picture, they get to make decisions, their actions make a difference for the future of the organization. Not so for the "lower" classes. Process centering washes away these feudal relics.

A process-centered organization is not an egalitarian one. Not everyone produces and performs the same. But it is one in which results, not status, count. "Workers" can make more than "managers" (though neither of these terms has much meaning anymore); everyone has to know what is going on in order to get his or her job done; decisions are made as close to the action as possible; and the most important people are those who create the most value. This is much more than just a fashionable inversion of the organizational chart to put customers and those who serve them at the top. It is the negation of the very notion of top, an affirmation that work rather than position is what really counts.

What title will I have?

Organizations of professionals use very few titles. A doctor is a doctor. A lawyer in a law firm is either an associate or a partner. Process-centered organizations are no exception; people who work in them are likely to go through their whole careers with only a single title or two. Moreover, the titles that people have will describe their professions rather than their ranks in some pecking order. That's what professional titles are for. If you have a bad case of acne, you want a dermatologist rather than a heart surgeon. Similarly, when you're putting together a process team, it's helpful to know whether someone is a financial analyst or an engineer. But beyond that there is little valuable information contained in the label that an organization affixes to you. Some process-centered organizations have even abolished titles altogether.

While it is very good to get rid of unnecessary titles, we can't dismiss them as totally unimportant. The truth is that titles play an enormously important role in providing people with psychic income. In fact, this is really why most people are concerned about titles in the first place.

People need to have their contributions acknowledged, and titles are one way of filling that need. They are external indicators and validators of a person's importance. They convey badges of achievement. But the price that we pay for titles—in the form of false distinctions and dysfunctional barriers—is just too high. This area is one of the great challenges that companies must overcome in moving to a process focus. If they eliminate managerial layers, how will they publicly recognize the achievements of outstanding workers? There are precedents for this question in fields ranging from the military to sports. It's not the negligible economic value of the ribbon and metal that makes a soldier proud of his Congressional Medal of Honor. A football player who's made a great play gets a sticker to paste on his helmet, a sticker that has no material value but is worth a fortune to the player. Businesses will have to learn how to use such intangible rewards as well.

What sort of future can I expect?

If titles and the promotions associated with them disappear, what will be the trajectory of a career? The simplest way to describe it is to say that the ladder is replaced by a series of concentric circles. Instead of being promoted from one job to a more "senior" one, your career is about personal growth, about doing more and doing it better. If you are a GTE customer care advocate, your career will be about becoming a better and more proficient CCA, handling ever-changing and more complex customer problems, handling more of them, and contributing in new ways to improve the company's relations with its customers. If you are a production worker at Monsanto, your goal is not to become a foreman but to become a better production worker. And the better you are, the more you will produce and the more you will be paid.

This does not mean that you will work in the same process for your entire life. An engineer may start out working in product development, spend some time in customer service, and then do a turn in order fulfillment. Throughout, however, he or she remains an engineer. This variety is almost certainly necessary to prevent people from going stale, but it has little to do with the conventional route of leaving engineering behind in order to get promoted into management.

Initially, such a future may not seem very exciting or interesting. But in many ways it offers far more hope and fulfillment than traditional career paths. Despite the optimism of youth, the reality is that only a mere handful of people rise to the top of a company. If success is defined as getting to the top, then everyone else is condemned to failure and frustration. But when success is defined not as putting yourself into the position of commanding others but of achieving the highest level of professional growth and personal performance of which you are capable, then everyone can be a success. The army recruiting slogan "Be all that you can be" is a good description of a process-centered career model.

One company where the managerial ladder is no longer the only route to personal success is Commerce Clearing House. CCH has established three separate career tracks: one for writers, one for product specialists and technology experts, and one for business leaders. As a result, writers and engineers are no longer forced to become managers in order to increase their salary. They can fashion a career that meets their financial goals while remaining in the disciplines in which they excel. The leadership track is for those (relatively few) people whose talents lie in leading and helping others. The company stresses that the leadership track is not preferred or better in any way, and it has adjusted compensation levels accordingly.

All three tracks are essentially equivalent, and all lead to well-paid positions. Since a great technologist can make just as much money as a great leader or a great writer at the summit of those tracks, people are urged to make their career choices based on what they enjoy and what they are best at doing, not on what it will pay. "We want you to come to work in the morning feeling like you're going to do something meaningful and fun," says Hugh Yarrington, head of CCH's Knowledge Organization. Yarrington urges people to move about, even try being a leader for a while to see how they like that. "It won't end your career if you don't."

In summary, in the process-centered world of work, you will need to be a professional with a professional education and attitude. You will be paid for what you produce. You may never get a high-status title because your career will see you growing laterally rather than climbing a corporate ladder. It will be an exciting, fulfilling, and rewarding world for those of today's workers who become professionals. The vital question you should be asking yourself is this: Are you ready to be one of them?

One way to assess your readiness is to reflect on the questions you would ask if you were called tomorrow to an interview for such a position. Would you ask how much the job pays? Would you inquire about promotions? The questions you ask reveal a great deal about yourself, and these questions can indicate a troublesome point of view.

In the process-centered business, *jobs* don't pay anything. Workers who produce results *earn* rewards. This is not just a word game: The words reflect mutually exclusive conceptions of what produces value and how compensation is acquired. The very idea of getting paid is an antiquated one. It suggests that jobs come with entitlements to a certain amount of income. In the old days, that may have been true. But not anymore. "Getting paid" makes sense only if you believe in a magical green pile from which you can be doled a share. In reality money comes from the customers, and they hand it over only if you create the value that they want.

The question "How can I be promoted?" is also obsolete. The concept of a promotion is something that advances you in a hierarchy. People in traditional companies are afflicted with an escalator mentality that assumes that as long as you don't do something extraordinarily bad, you can get ahead just by standing still. In process-centered companies, the escalator has become a rope ladder. Progress, growth, new opportunities, and higher income come through improved performance, which takes constant learning and hard work. The professional does not ask about promotion. He asks, instead, "What does it take to succeed?"

A professional approaches a company by asking questions about its goals and attitudes rather than its pension plan and vacation schedules. "What is your strategy?" "What makes you better than your competition?" These demonstrate a recognition that your success depends on the company's and that there are no winners on a losing team. This is the attitude of someone who's ready for the process-centered world.

To some people, the professional jobs in a process-centered company seem like great fun. They may be demanding but they are also highly rewarding. After years of mind-numbing busywork, many people feel that these jobs will finally allow them to enjoy life in the fast lane. But for others, the freedom is terrifying and the new responsibilities seem filled with peril. To them, this isn't life in the fast lane—it's playing in traffic.

Over the past few years I have asked thousands of people attending my seminars how these new jobs actually feel to the people who perform them. The striking thing about the responses has been their polarity.

Many people blurt out the word "exciting." They say they can't wait to go to work Monday mornings. "We thought we'd died and gone to heaven," said one person speaking for a group of co-workers. These people describe their process jobs as by far the best they've ever had. Work has become the most fulfilling part of their lives. Work is exciting because no two days are exactly the same. The wide range of situations they encounter and the creativity they must apply to deal with these situations make work a constantly changing kaleidoscope. "I'm never bored," says Anna Wilson, a customer care advocate at GTE. "Every day has new challenges and new opportunities to learn." Another individual says, "I used to do things because I had to; now I want to."

The new application-handling process at Aetna Life & Casualty has transformed the attitudes of the people involved in it. The people who are the most energized and enthusiastic are those who had formerly been lowest on the totem pole: the processing clerks. These people, who had been little more than paper pushers, now have the satisfaction of knowing that they are making a real difference. They feel respected for what they do—and with good reason. They and their work truly matter.

But one person's relief at being freed from the bridle is another's feeling of being overwhelmed by too many choices. Some people are more comfortable being told what to do and letting someone else take both the responsibility and the heat. For them, a process-centered world is one in which clarity and order have given way to anxiety and uncertainty.

One company interviewed a group of its employees seeking their opinions of the new process environment in which they were now working. Most were enthusiastic—but not all. "There aren't enough supervisors around," said one. "I don't like having to make my own decisions. They don't pay me enough for that."

Everyone who has served in the military knows that despite the privileges afforded officers and their greater freedom to make decisions, many enlisted personnel turn down the opportunity to attend Officer Candidate School. In fact, some of them turn it down precisely because of the freedom it conveys. Freedom involves ambiguity, and for some people the payoff isn't worth it.

To put it another way, in a process-centered environment some people will feel excited by empowerment and visibility while others will feel tormented and frazzled by exposure. When performance is measured objectively and you have direct responsibility, you can't pass the buck or duck the blame. For better or worse, you and your work can be seen by all. There's no anonymity and no place to hide.

Professional and entrepreneurial life is life on the edge. It is far more demanding than just plodding along and following the rules. So it isn't surprising that many people find it *both* exciting and frazzling. Professionals are far more prone to overwork and burnout than people who work at narrow traditional jobs, because their jobs have no built-in limits. For professionals, there's no five o'clock whistle. Work is not a job but part of one's life. Engineers who are up to their eyes solving problems are probably happy to have the opportunity to do the work they chose for their careers, but being intellectually challenged all day and every day is likely to be bone-tiring. One person described his process-centered job as follows: "I'm having the most fun of my life, but after two years of sixty-hour weeks, I'm tired."

William Faulkner once observed that you can't eat, drink, or make love all day; the only thing you can do all day is work. A process-centered environment takes this to extremes. Meaningful and interesting work gets its hooks into you and may never let go. Moreover, knowing that harder work can generate increased earnings can nag people with the ultimately destructive thought that they might do better for themselves if

they never went home at all. It's not a coincidence that entrepreneurs have an extraordinarily high divorce rate.

Progressive Insurance's COO, Bruce Marlow, observes that
the company's adjusters used to be able to say that they were
white-collar professionals who worked in a nice office park
from nine to five on weekdays. "But under the new situation,
you can't schedule your work and you don't work nine to
five. People work different shifts, and when a claim comes in,
you go to the scene of that accident. It requires a lot more
commitment." It's also a tougher way to live.

Removing limits on what people can achieve can be a perverse invitation to burnout. It is exhilarating to be stretched to
your limit, but after a while you need a break before *you*
break. All-day, every-day stimulation can fry your nerves like
wiring that carries too much current. And if work is the
source of your greatest personal fulfillment, what happens to
the rest of your life? Where are you to find the energy for
family, hobbies, and community? Is such work fun or is it
misery? People in a process-centered world need to remind
themselves of the old saw that few people on their deathbeds
wish they'd spent more time at the office.

While entrepreneurs are the quintessential American folk
heroes, they are also driven people. We admire the entrepreneur's ingenuity, creativity, and stick-to-itiveness. An entrepreneurial spirit energizes a workplace with a can-do atmosphere
and an obsession with providing customer value. But this
spirit is at its heart based in fear. Scratch most entrepreneurs
and you'll find at least a trace of panic in their bloodstreams.
They live in constant dread of being overwhelmed by larger
competitors or supplanted by newer ones. Process professionals live lives similarly balanced between exhilaration and anxiety, between fulfillment and fear.

Most aspects of a process-centered environment can be
judged only subjectively, reflecting each individual's personal

value system and attitudes. But there is one objective fact: In a process-centered world, there is no job security.

Fred Musone is president of Morton International Automotive Safety Products. He tells his people that he can't give them job security and neither can a union contract. The customer alone is in a position to do that, and the customer is a notoriously demanding and fickle taskmaster. The customer has loyalty only to value, and the customer's expectations are constantly rising—which is why entrepreneurs sleep so poorly.

The new pact that a company offers process professionals centers on providing the *opportunity* to perform by creating value for the customer. Creating value will enable people to develop their careers and attain ample rewards. But the company and the individual have little further commitment to each other. If business conditions change, the company has made no promises to the professional. Conversely, if a better personal opportunity presents itself elsewhere, the professional need feel no obligation to remain with the company. Apple Computer already tells its people that they should not assume they'll spend their entire careers at that particular oasis. It may happen, of course, but no one should count on it.

As process-centered organizations adopt the styles and behavioral modes of entrepreneurial firms, their flexibility and performance improve dramatically. But these gains are purchased with the higher levels of anxiety and stress that are the unspoken ingredients of entrepreneurial success.

In short, one certain feature of your future, and of everyone else's too, is . . . uncertainty. The work you do today may not exist next year, and your company may not exist five years hence.

Process-centered work transforms workers into professionals, with all the advantages and disadvantages this implies. But the transformation of work and workers also requires the transformation of managers. That is our next concern.

PART II

MANAGEMENT

CHAPTER 5

FROM MANAGER TO PROCESS OWNER

OUR DISCUSSION so far has focused on the changing nature of work and workers in the process-centered organization. We have seen how work moves from a task focus to a process emphasis and how in so doing workers become process professionals. But what of managers? We have not yet had much to say about the nature and role of management jobs in the process-centered enterprise.

This is unusual (most business books begin and end with management) but fitting. We are breaking with the traditional management-centered organization in which workers are by and large positioned as drones, trained to carry out the instructions of their superiors and (presumably) betters. In such a company, workers are believed to be as interchangeable as the parts they're handling, and so successes and failures are inevitably attributed to the caliber of its management. In the process-centered organization, by contrast, the people who make the most difference are the people who directly create value for the customer. They come first, and so they have in our discussion. Work is more important than management, and so must precede it. It is only now that we turn our attention to the manager.

Two basic questions should underlie any serious consideration of the nature of management. The first is "*What* do managers manage?" and the second is "*Why* do managers manage?" The answers to both are changing.

Let's start with the "why." In general, a manager is someone who does the things that workers cannot do for themselves. Since in the traditional view workers were assumed to be simple, unreliable, and of limited educability, the role prescribed for management was very large indeed. If workers lack the intellectual ability to do more than the most routine of activities and, if left to their own devices, they work neither reliably nor hard, then the manager, the supervisor, the overseer plays the key role in the company—ensuring that workers do the right thing.

Whether or not these assumptions about workers were ever accurate, companies were organized as though they were and thus created self-fulfilling prophecies. If you treat people like irresponsible drones, eventually they will start behaving like them. But these assumptions are completely at odds with the principles of the process-centered organization. The notion of simple workers inevitably leads to small and narrow jobs that must be tightly overseen by supervisory managers. The inevitable consequence of this is that the organization's processes will perforce be highly complex, pieced together out of innumerable small jobs and burdened with an extensive supervisory superstructure. These complex processes will, of course, be costly, rigid, and error-prone.

Today we must start at the other end of this deductive

chain. We must have high performing processes—simple, lean, low cost, and flexible. Such processes must be based on jobs that are broad and big, which in turn means there is no place in the new organization for the presumed drones that populated the old one. We simply must have workers capable of performing process-focused jobs, jobs that demand understanding, autonomy, responsibility, and decision making. Such workers do not need supervision, so the need for the traditional manager no longer exists.

We are also experiencing a shift in the *object* of a manager's attention. If one had asked a traditional manager what he or she actually managed, the answer would usually have been the name of a department—a group of people performing a particular activity. The manager was there to look after the work of the department, assuring that it was correctly performed. He or she would obtain the resources (human and financial) required by the department, determine that they were well used, and attend to the personal and developmental needs of the department personnel. One part controller, one part supervisor, one part baby-sitter: that was the recipe for the traditional manager. The department was the basic building block of the organization and the basic unit of managerial attention. All other managerial roles were layered on top of the departmental manager.

This model is no longer tenable in the age of customers and processes. Now that companies must be designed and focused for the benefit of customers, the mechanisms that create and deliver value to them must be the organization's basic units and therefore the primary focus of managerial attention. These, of course, are the organization's processes. The departmental manager must give way to a new role, that of the process owner—an individual concerned with assuring not the performance of a department's tasks but the successful realization of a complete end-to-end process.

The term "process owner" has its antecedents in the quality

movement and has already achieved some currency, which is why we use it. But it does suffer from two drawbacks. First, some people equate the term with a temporary project manager, someone whose short-term responsibility is to address and fix a process's performance problems. Our definition of a process owner includes those duties but goes far beyond them; we see the role as permanent and vital. Second, labeling one individual as the "owner" of a process might seem to absolve all others of responsibility for it. In fact, as we have seen, all the people performing a process must have some ownership of it and share responsibility for its successful outcome. It is in the person of the process owner, however, that this responsibility is most precisely located. It is where Harry Truman's buck eventually stops. Perhaps for these reasons, a number of companies are using other terms: "process leader," "process manager," or even "process martyr" (not a recommended term). Charles Dunagan, a vice president of Shell Chemical Company who is owner of the customer order and inquiry fulfillment process there, describes himself as "someone who spends his time thinking about work and processes. My job is linking tasks into one body of work and then looking at the complete process and making sure that it all works together."

But what exactly does this entail? What can the performers of a process, clever as they are, not do for themselves? The answer to this question will change over time, since the capabilities of the process performers will evolve. In the early years of a company's transition to process centering, the people performing a process will still be burdened with the limitations they developed under the old regime. As they develop new skills and attitudes, the responsibilities of the process owner will diminish; in effect, as process performers themselves better adjust to the process environment, they can assume more of the owner's role. In general, however, we can break down the process owner's responsibility into three major areas: design, coaching, and advocacy.

Design

Imagine that a company convenes a team of individuals who are to perform a product development process: perhaps some engineers, a marketing expert, someone with manufacturing expertise, some people from finance, and the like. They are ready and eager to begin work. Each is skilled in his or her individual domain. But how shall they perform the process? What are they to do to get a product developed? While they must be autonomous and empowered to proceed without the heavy hand of a stultifying bureaucracy, someone does need to tell them how to develop products, the steps that must be taken, and the order in which they should be performed. Empowerment does not equal anarchy; every process team cannot, as the Bible scornfully has it, "do what is right in their eyes." It is not reasonable to expect a process team to improvise the process as they perform it. It is the process owner's responsibility to provide the team with the knowledge of the process so they can perform it. The process owner "owns" not the performance of the process but its design, sharing it with all the teams who perform it. Thus the process owner has responsibility for the design of the process and its documentation, and for training process performers in its structure and conduct.

Before the process owner can instruct performers in the structure and design of the process, this design must exist. Creating and maintaining it is the first of the owner's responsibilities. It is for the owner to find and formulate the best way of filling orders, developing products, or resolving customer complaints, and then make sure that it remains the best way.

While processes exist in conventional organizations, they only rarely have been consciously designed. They are usually the accretions of endless ad hoc decisions that have been made over time in response to changing circumstances. Consequently they usually perform very poorly. One of the major motivations organizations have for moving to process centering is to get their processes under control by ensuring that they do in fact have well thought out and documented designs. While process design is not a one-person activity, the responsibility for it sits on the process owner's shoulders.

Traditionally, design was something associated only with products. It is now critical in processes as well. While not yet a science, process design can fairly be termed an engineering discipline. Like all branches of engineering, it requires grounding in a set of basic principles and techniques as well as a facility for design, for creating well-fashioned structures, and for recognizing the advantages and flaws of alternative schemes. Positioning process ownership as a serious form of engineering forces us to reposition management as a respectable discipline in which substantive education does make a difference. One would not ask someone off the street to design a computer or an automobile. Why should such a person be expected to design a process?

Process design must take place in a framework of principles, and the first principle is that process design must be customer-driven. If processes exist to create value for customers then it follows that they should create the kinds of values that customers want in the ways that they want them. So process design must begin by formulating a customer-driven, outside-in perspective on the performance requirements of the process. What should the process really provide its customers? How much are customers willing to pay for the result of the process? How quickly do they need it? How much flexibility do they demand? What degree of precision is required? It is the process owner's responsibility to obtain answers to these questions from both existing and prospective customers.

If the process is to perform well, "well" must be precisely defined in a way that is measurable, unambiguous, understood by everyone involved, and relatable to people's own work. For instance, one measure of the performance of an order fulfillment process might be "percent of perfect orders": the fraction of orders that are filled "perfectly," that is, on time, correctly, and completely. By understanding customers' needs, the process owner identifies this as a key measure for the process as a whole, while also specifying the target level of performance (i.e., the precise percentage) that the process must achieve. He or she also breaks down this overall measure into a "measurement architecture," a related set of narrower performance measures that are more directly associated with the work performed by individuals. The person entering the order into the computer system, the warehouse worker reordering inventory, the traffic planner selecting the best mode of delivery—each affects the overall performance measure, each must be held accountable for it, but each is somewhat removed from it. The warehouse worker needs a performance measure that's more completely within his personal control, one that he can connect to and that will directly shape his personal behavior. The process owner may, for instance, ascertain that out-of-stock situations in the warehouse lead to late deliveries, and so defines for the warehouse worker a performance measure that revolves around such shortfall contingencies and sets a particular target to shoot for.

In addition to meeting customer requirements, the process owner must also establish measures that meet the *company's* needs: for profitability, return on assets, growth, and the like. Going broke while satisfying customers is not a viable strategy. The process owner must balance customer needs with company needs and create a design that meets both.

Establishing process designs and performance targets is not a static responsibility for the process owner but an ongoing and dynamic one. Over time, customer requirements and technology capabilities may change. It is the process owner's continuing design responsibility to see that the process keeps up with the one and exploits the other. To do this, the process owner must keep an ear to the ground, detecting when the existing design needs improvement in order to remain competitive. Ongoing customer communications, benchmarking of both competitors and other companies, and engaging process performers in a dialogue about their problems and perceptions are some of the mechanisms the process owner employs in this regard.

Having recognized that the time has come to update the process, the owner must convene a redesign effort to change it. Such efforts come in two flavors: incremental and radical. Incremental redesign means modifying the process to solve problems that prevent it from attaining the required performance level. Eliminating unproductive activities or changing the means by which a task is performed are typical incremental process changes that lead to the small improvements in performance that are usually sufficient to keep a process competitive. Periodically, however, there is a more dramatic change in the world: The old design suddenly becomes obsolete, an entirely new measure becomes important, or a quantum leap is required in an existing one. In such circumstances incremental change to the process design is not enough, and the process owner must replace the existing design with an entirely new one. Figure 1 illustrates this ongoing and endless cycle of process improvement that is conducted by the process owner. (For the cognoscenti of the quality movement, this is clearly derived from Shewhart and Deming's Plan/Do/Check/Act cycle.)

In the process-centered organization, this program of process improvement is not a secondary and peripheral activity. It is the essence of management. The process-centered organization embodies the notion that one manages a business not by managing budgets, departments, or people but by managing processes. In fact, I submit that the notion that people can and need to be managed is feudal and disrespectful. People need to be treated like the responsible and autonomous

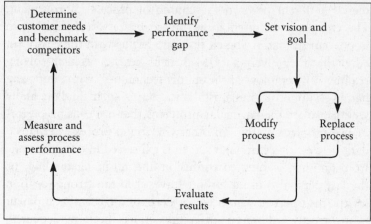

Figure 1

individuals that they are. If they are given the information and tools that they need to perform, if they are provided with an understanding of customer requirements and of the big picture of the work, if they are guided by clear measurement systems, and if they are treated with respect, then they will do what needs to be done without being "managed." It is the processes, the inert designs of work, that need management and oversight—not people.

The terms we have used—incremental redesign and radical redesign—are more popularly known as TQM and reengineering. Over the last five years these two schools of process improvement have been the subject of a debate approaching theological warfare in its intensity. Some people have argued that the two were in fact the same, that reengineering was merely old quality wine in new bottles. Others felt that reengineering, with its top-down and radical orientation, was incompatible with the bottom-up and milder approach of TQM. Still others felt that the two were competitors and that organizations needed to choose one or the other.

While it is easy to sympathize with those who hold such views, they are all incorrect. Reengineering and TQM are merely different pews in the church of process improvement. The two share an orientation toward process, a dedication to improvement, and a dogma that one begins with the customer. After that they diverge. TQM is at its heart a problem-solving regimen. It employs a host of techniques with imposing names—Pareto diagrams, Ishikawa charts—that fundamentally seek to isolate the particular problems that are causing performance problems within an otherwise sound process. Perhaps a data field on one computer screen is expressed in different units from another, leading to confusion and misunderstanding, or the last person to use a forklift leaves it in the wrong location for the next person who needs it. Perhaps a piece of equipment is incorrectly calibrated, or a person has been inadequately trained. TQM rigorously traces the symptoms of an inadequately performing process back to such "root causes," highlighting the underlying problem so that it can be addressed. When the "performance gap" between the performance of a process and what is required of it is small, then such problem-solving techniques are called for. However, large gaps cannot be filled by tinkering. TQM assumes that the design of the process is sound and that all it needs is some minor enhancement. But if the world has changed dramatically since the process was first (or most recently) designed, the current design may be fundamentally flawed and incapable of delivering the required performance. Reengineering is then called for. Reengineering does not merely enhance the individual steps of the process but entirely reconsiders how they are put together.

Figure 2 illustrates how TQM and reengineering fit together over time in the life story of a process. First, the process is enhanced until its useful lifetime is over, at which point it is reengineered. Then, enhancement is resumed and the entire cycle starts again. Note this means that reengineering is not a once-in-a-lifetime endeavor. As we have already observed, the reengineering revolution has had two major themes: The first is concerned with aligning organizations around their processes,

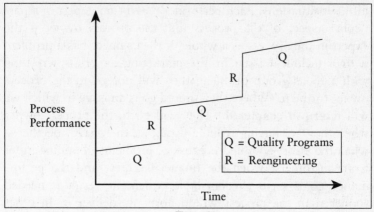

Figure 2

while the second focuses on replacing existing process designs with superior ones. The first of these is in fact a one-time shift in an organization's philosophy and self-perspective, but the latter must be a never-ending struggle. As business circumstances change in major ways, so must process designs.

In the context of their design responsibility, process owners also have control of the automation efforts that support the process. Conventionally, computerization efforts have been as fragmented as the organizations they are intended to support. Systems have been built to meet the needs of the marketing department, the warehouse, or the order entry group, but never for the end-to-end order fulfillment process. The simple reason is that there has been no one to speak for the process. That role now falls to the process owner, who holds the purse strings and calls the shots on how technology should be deployed on behalf of the process.

Coaching

Once process performers have been trained in the process design, the process owner is available to help them through difficult situations. Each performer may be an expert in a particular aspect of the process, but the process owner is the expert in the process as a whole. If the engineer has a problem with a technical issue or the marketing expert is wrestling with a focus group problem, they will *not* go to the process owner for help. (Where they should go is an issue to which we will return in chapter 8.) They will go to the process owner when they are having trouble fitting all the pieces together— when the effort is stalled because of problems obtaining input from customers, when the financial targets and the performance goals seem irreconcilable, when the result is needed sooner than the process would normally deliver it. In other words, the team goes to the process owner when they have trouble making the process design work in their particular situation and need some help adapting it to exceptional circumstances. The process owner's expertise, to return to Charles Dunagan's term, is in "linking tasks into one body of work . . . and making sure that it all works together." Even if all the process performers have the big picture, the process owner has the biggest picture of all.

Team breakdowns are a particular source of process-performance problems with which the process owner will have to contend. Since process work is often teamwork, process owners need to be able to facilitate it. Despite the current popularity of the team concept, most people in contemporary organizations have virtually no experience working in teams (though many have some experience playing on them). One does not make a group of individuals into a team simply by declaring them to be one. It takes training and learning, and even then the path is not an easy one. There will inevitably be friction and conflicts among process team members, even if they are all agreed on the ultimate objectives of the process and are measured by the same yardstick. Personality differences, legitimate divergences in opinion, tension, and stress—these are but a few of the realities that can cause a team to get stuck. It would be nice to think that mature individuals will be able to see past petty problems and resolve them unaided, but just as Freud taught us that it is virtually impossible to psychoanalyze oneself (Freud himself being the notable exception), so it is hard for a team to overcome its own breakdowns. The process owner has to step into the breach and help. The key word here is "help." It avails little if the process owner immediately intervenes to "solve" the problem; that should be the solution of last resort, since it is "disempowering" in the worst way. The process owner should be a guide and a facilitator, not "the boss." It is only when all else fails that the process owner takes things into his or her own hands.

Cynics may claim that the coaching aspect of a process owner's job is just a linguistic trick, that it is nothing more than the old supervisory role. Nothing could be further from the truth. First, the process owner does not hover over the team, checking on their performance. He or she does monitor their results and investigate if there are problems, but absent such problems the process owner only gets involved if the team members approach him. He does not check or supervise; he is a resource to be drawn upon when needed. Second, the relationship between the process owner and the process performers is fundamentally different from the old relationship between supervisors and workers. The departmental manager was typically selected because he or she was the best at doing the actual work of the department: the best sales rep became sales manager, the star engineer became an engineering supervisor. This was consistent with the duties of the supervisory manager, namely assuring the correct performance of the department's tasks. If the manager had enough time, he or she could, in fact, have performed all the department's work alone. As it was, the manager unfortunately had to have subordinates who would perform what rightly should have been the manager's own work. The workers were the manager's arms and legs, or even fingers and toes, but the intelligence all resided with the manager.

This model is irrelevant to the process owner. The owner of the product development process could *not* develop products entirely on his or her own. In fact, the owner of the product development process might only be barely qualified to perform *any* of the specific tasks associated with product development. The process owner is a linker, a facilitator, an enabler of those who actually do the work. It would be more accurate to say that he reports to the performers—since he is on call, at their disposal—than to say that they work for him.

If the old managerial structure was the "glue" that held the old fragmented organization together, the process owner in his coaching role can be likened to the "oil" that lubricates the performance of process performers to ensure that they are effective. By helping them in exceptional situations, providing them with the knowledge and tools they require, assisting them in resolving conflicts, and redeploying resources when necessary, the process owner ensures that they are free to exercise their skills in making the process work.

Advocacy

The performers carry out the process, but the owner represents it. It is the owner's job to obtain the financial resources that the process needs in order to operate. It is these resources that will fund the performers, the tools, and the facilities they require. More fundamentally, the process owner has a seat at what is becoming known as the process council. This group, typically consisting of the leader of the business, the process owners, and the heads of key support groups, provides a context for transcending individual processes and addressing the needs of the business as a whole. It would be tragic if functional silos were to be replaced by process tunnels, if the old fragmentation into departmental dukedoms were merely to give way to process protectorates that are defended with equal jealousy. A business is not just a group of processes, it is a *system* of processes that must interact to create all the results customers need. Without product development, order fulfillment has nothing to deliver, and without order fulfillment, the results of product development sit on the shelf. It is critical that individual processes be integrated, that their boundaries mesh smoothly, that they cooperate rather than conflict. The process council is the mechanism for achieving this.

Perhaps the most critical requirement for this council is that it operate as a team. It is an unfortunate reality that many managers live by a different set of rules than those they apply to their subordinates. This is one of the great sources of corporate cynicism. If process performers must work as teams, so must the process owners when they meet in council. It is natural—and even desirable—that each process owner try to get as much support as possible for his or her process and try to get others to adapt to its needs rather than the other way around. But this narrow perspective must be tempered by a concern for the organization as a whole, by shared rather than individual objectives. It is not enough for the processes to perform individually; they must perform together, which will require adjustment on everyone's part. It is only through real teamwork that the process council can make this a reality. In doing so they set a useful example for the rest of the organization. To quote Albert Schweitzer, "When it comes to teaching values, example isn't the best way—it's the only way."

Clearly the process owners will have their hands full designing and redesigning the process, coaching the process teams, and representing it in the corridors of power. Process ownership is unlikely to be a one-person job. At the very least, the process owner must be supported by the process performers in the ongoing improvement effort. Despite his or her talents, the process owner suffers from one serious disadvantage: He or she is not actually performing the process on the front lines. The process owner may have perspective but lacks immediacy. Therefore, the owner must maintain close communication ties with the performers to know what is happening, what is working and what is not, and when it is time for a change. GTE, for instance, appoints a panel of performers for each process. These individuals spend most of their time working the process, but 10 to 15 percent of their time is occupied with identifying areas of needed improvement and developing ways to address them. The process owner is also likely to have a supporting technical staff who assist in the training, measurement, and redesign activities for which the process owner has responsibility. If there are a great many teams performing a process, one individual cannot provide them with all the coaching they may need, so the process owner will need assistance here too. If the process is large and complex, it may be necessary to break it down into subprocesses, each of which will have an owner in turn. But none of this should be confused with a conventional hierarchy. Process ownership is itself a process. If there is more to do than one person can handle then a team is called for. While one of these individuals may be nominally "in charge," the work is a collective responsibility of the process ownership team, just as is the case for any other process team.

The process owner role is not a prospective one; it is here. In 1995, we conducted a survey of fifty large multinational sponsors of our Phoenix research consortium. Of these corporations, thirty-nine had already introduced the process-owner role and the rest were beginning to do so. As is inevitable in the early days of any concept, terminology is far from standard and there are significant variations in the role. But companies from Delco and Ford to Bell Atlantic and AT&T, just to name a few, are committed to process ownership as a central theme in organizing and managing their enterprises.

Companies do not typically decide overnight that process ownership is the solution to all their problems. Rather, executives typically start down this road by recognizing that the existing processes are performing poorly and that their cross-functional nature means that no one is responsible for improving them. Thus the first incarnation of the process owner is a project manager for a process improvement effort, either reengineering or TQM. Initially the process owner functions much like a brand manager in a consumer products company. Without having direct control over the organization's resources, he has to bring together many disparate aspects of the company to achieve a single objective. At this stage in development, the process owner is in effect overlaid on the existing (functional) organizational structure, operating through influence rather than authority. It is the traditional management hierarchy that still holds the reins.

Before long, however, the company realizes that the benefits of the improvement program will not last unless there is an ongoing capability to maintain and enhance them, which in turn means that the process owner role must be institutionalized. As one executive has put it, "We realized we couldn't operate the new process in the old organization." This is the point at which the pendulum of power begins to move toward the process owner; the process owner becomes a "line" decision maker rather than a staff coordinator. As a recognition of the centrality of processes further permeates the organization, the authority of the preexisting structure begins to diminish. Process comes to the fore and the process owner becomes the primary managerial role.

As should be clear by now, the relationship between process owner and process performer is not that of manager and subordinate, of foreman and laborer. Process owners are light-years away from the supervisors and middle managers they replace; process owners are enablers, not bosses or straw bosses. A process performer might be said to work for the customer, or maybe for himself, but certainly not for the process owner. The latter's role is neither heroic nor modest, it is merely essential. The process owner provides the performers with the wherewithal they require to accomplish their mission. The glory in a process-centered organization belongs more to those who do the work than to those who help. To those readers who are even now contemplating how they could get promoted into one of these process owner jobs, my response is "Are you sure you want it?" In a traditional organization managers are the winners, the ones with the highest incomes and the highest status. In a process-centered organization the people who contribute the most, who create the greatest value, are the winners. To be sure, process owners can be winners, but they're not the only ones who can.

The end of the manager's monopoly on status is more than compensated for by the process owner's newfound ability to take real pride in his own work. What real glory was there in being a "manager," whose highest credential is to be called a Master of Business *Administration*? An administrator is almost the worst thing one can call a person. It evokes the image of a petty bureaucrat, a paper shuffler out of touch with the substance of business and work. What clarity or pride is there in it? The process owner role is grounded in contribution, not a position on a chart. "I make sure that customers' orders are filled correctly and on time," is a lot better thing to tell your children than "I check on people to make sure they're not screwing up."

The role of the process owner is easy to describe, but very difficult to fill. The job requires an individual with an exceedingly diverse set of talents and capabilities. The process owner must have a broad knowledge of the process, an intuition for the needs of customers, and a holistic perspective that lets him or her think broadly about the process rather than about its individual constituents. A process owner must have the engineering skills to measure, diagnose, and design the process; the interpersonal skills to coach the performers carrying out the process; and the political skills to advocate for it. As one company has put it, "It's a person who knows how to coach and counsel and help, knows how to get resources and how to remove obstructions, and who is capable of engendering a lot of loyalty and hard work."

Becoming a process owner, however, involves even more than acquiring new skills and attitudes. It involves abandoning old ways of managing. For traditional management cadres, reared in a culture of control and oversight, this means that they must relinquish the practices that have made them successful. Among other things, they must learn to let people make mistakes so that they can learn from them instead of immediately intervening to ensure the right outcome, to deflect requests for instructions by asking the petitioner what he or she thinks should be done, and to take pride in influencing people through knowledge and respect rather than by controlling them via a reporting structure. These are unnatural attitudes for the traditional hands-on, can-do manager.

In a way it is fortunate that the demands on process owners are so high, since we don't need very many of them. There are only a modest number of processes in even the largest companies, even when one includes all the subprocesses. In a multibillion-dollar enterprise, there may be anywhere from fifty to one hundred processes all told. This does not mean a lot of available chairs for today's managers when the old music stops. Even large processes, which are performed by many teams and so need a lot of coaches, are not long-term havens for today's managers. As process teams develop more familiarity with the process, as they enhance their abilities to solve their own problems, less intervention will be needed from the process owners, and so fewer people will be required to provide it.

This reduction in the number of managers is an unalloyed good for the company. Managers—even process owners—are by definition non-value-adding; the work they do may be important and necessary, but it is not work for which the customer is willing to pay. Management is a necessary evil, and the less of it that is needed, the better. The individual manager, however, may be forgiven for not sharing this sanguine outlook. Process ownership is a role for which he or she is likely to be untrained and emotionally unsuited. Some managers will be able to retool themselves for the new positions that a process-centered organization offers, but some will not. For those who do, the rewards will be considerable. The process owner is the nexus of the organization, knitting together all aspects of the process to make sure that the results are produced. There is real satisfaction, real contribution, and real reward in making this happen.

Process centering starts a chain reaction that affects everyone from the frontline performer to the CEO. Not only are old roles either eliminated or transformed beyond recognition, but entirely new ones, like process owner, come into being. If there were a section in the Smithsonian for antiquated artifacts of the American economy, the conventional manager would be the subject of a large display case.

Process has triumphed over task, vision over supervision. In this and preceding chapters we have examined many aspects of the demise of the old order and the rise of the new. But a piece-by-piece look is not entirely sufficient. The ideas we have presented must be organized into a coherent whole; without the big picture, the details don't fit together. In the next chapter we will consider such a framework.

Yet theories are also insufficient. Bright and clear as they can be, they lack flesh and blood, the tang of experience. In the end we always want to relate the unknown to something with which we are familiar. Therefore, after spending some time in the rarefied world of theory, we'll get back down to earth—in fact to some of the world's least theoretical patches of turf, the gridirons of the National Football League.

CHAPTER 6

WHAT IS BUSINESS ANYWAY?

WHEN WORLD WAR II ended, Pan American World Airways had 100 percent of America's Pacific market, 90 percent of the Caribbean market, and nearly a third of the transatlantic market. By 1991 its share had dwindled to nothing; Pan Am was gone.

In 1981 Wang Laboratories, an esteemed pioneer in electronic calculators and word processors, was the eleventh largest U.S. computer company. Ten years later it barely existed.

Between 1987 and 1993 International Business Machines, once the nation's premier computer company, saw its customers flock to smaller rivals and the market value of its stock plunge $27 billion.

A practically endless list could be made of companies that have grown great and fallen—Bethlehem Steel, Eastern Airlines, Lockheed, and on and on. What happened to them?

How could they have been so successful and then suddenly lost their way? The truth is that most of them never really knew their way in the first place.

With a few exceptions like Alfred Sloan's General Motors, the vast industrial organizations that led this century's unprecedented economic growth weren't planned and built by design. They were boats luckily lifted by an incoming tide, and they had just enough agility to keep themselves from capsizing. One day an entrepreneur—whether Henry Ford or Bill Gates—would come up with a clever idea, right for the time; the next, he would be sitting astride a colossal Ford Motor or a Microsoft. Rather than managerial expertise, it was the genius and good fortune of the original visionary—plus exploding demand—that led to business success. Corporate managers may have thought they were smart, but actually they were just lucky. They were like someone who steps aboard the jungle cruise boat at Disney World, dons a yachting blazer and a nautical cap, spins the wheel, and imagines he's controlling the boat. In reality, the boat is being pulled by a cable, and he's just along for the ride. For many successful companies, the cable was exploding customer demand, and their managers were just guys in nautical caps. If managers really knew what they were about, business success would be a far less haphazard phenomenon than it has proven to be.

Business reversals of the scale and frequency we have seen in modern times cannot be attributed to extraordinary factors. Pan Am, Wang, and IBM had absolutely everything going for them: financial resources, loyal customers, market share, brand-name recognition, and more. Their leaders and staffs were neither incompetent nor ignorant. Why did they falter? Because the well-educated people running them weren't educated to think about the right things in the right way. All their vaunted expertise and knowledge was little more effective than blind luck in achieving and maintaining organizational success.

My own formal education is in three fields. I earned a bachelor's degree in mathematics, a master's in electrical engineering, and a doctorate in computer science. As a researcher and an academic I worked in a series of different technical areas. Each time I moved into a new one, I looked for what scientists call first principles: the basic concepts or theories that govern a field. Identifying and understanding these principles provide a framework for examining, interpreting, predicting, and even controlling events or actions within the field. Kirchhoff's laws characterize the behavior of electrical circuits, for example; Newton's laws of motion predict the behavior of objects in the physical world. However, when I approached the business world I found that it had no first principles. I looked for the underlying theory that would help me interpret and understand corporate management. I was dismayed to discover that there was none.

Businesspeople couldn't even agree on what a company was. It was like the proverbial blind men describing the elephant. Financial specialists maintained that a company was its balance sheet, capital structure, and cash flow. Manufacturing people described it in terms of plants, fixed assets, and production activities. To R&D specialists, a company was its technologies; to marketing people, its products. Senior corporate executives typically defined their companies in terms of strategy.

All those people, from technologists to CEOs, were grappling with the same fundamental question: What is a company? Eventually I decided that a useful theory of business—a set of first principles—might be surfaced by asking a different question.

This question originated with John Ciardi's book *How Does a Poem Mean?* The author explained his title by arguing that a poem's meaning is to be found not just in *what* is written but in how it is written—that is, its mode of expression.

Ciardi, a poet himself, argued that poetry's insights and literary devices are inseparable—"Each feeds the other." Taking a similar approach to business, the question "What is a company?" becomes "What is a company *for*?" or "Why is a company?" In other words, only after we determine the end purpose of a company—its reason for being—can we begin to shape an identity and structure to suit that purpose. To that end, let me propose a simple assertion.

Principle 1: The mission of a business is to create value for its customers

Why is a company? What is it for? I submit that the only useful contemporary answer is that a company exists to create customer value. Everything a company does must be directed to this end.

But what is a customer? The traditional definition is someone who buys what the company sells. But this is imprecise and incomplete. A better definition is that customers are people whose behavior the company wishes to influence by providing them with value. (By influence, incidentally, I don't mean "deceive"; deception is not a business practice, it is a criminal practice known as fraud.) This much broader definition is far more useful in today's increasingly complex commercial environment in which customers come in many varieties.

Consumer goods companies, for instance, have at least two kinds of customers: consumers—those who purchase and use the company's products—and retailers. In the one case, the company wishes to influence the consumer to select and use its products; in the second the company wants the retailer to carry its products, to allocate substantial shelf space to them, and to promote them in advertising.

The company-customer relationship can become very complex. Which among the following is a customer of a pharmaceutical company?

A. The patient who takes a medicine.
B. The physician who prescribes it.
C. The pharmacist who dispenses it.
D. The wholesaler who distributes it.
E. The Food and Drug Administration scientists and officials who approve its use.
F. The insurance company that pays for it.

The answer is: all of the above. They are all customers. Pharmaceutical companies must influence each and every one of these individuals and institutions.

How, then, do companies influence customer behavior? By creating value for them. The fundamental relationship between companies and customers may appear to be based on the exchange of products or services for money, but it is actually broader than that. The relationship is based on providing value in order to influence and shape behavior.

And what is value? Value is not synonymous with a product or service, although it often involves one or both. Rather, value in a business context means a solution to a customer's problem. It is whatever it takes to answer a customer's need, to scratch a customer's itch. Each of the drug company's customers requires a different value: the patient, an effective medication; the physician, information on when the medication should be used; the pharmacist, availability of product for sale; the FDA, data to enable the evaluation of the compound's effectiveness and safety. Each is solving a different problem, and the drug company needs to help each one do so.

Parenthetically we should also note that customers cannot always articulate in advance the value that they require from a company (although they are usually very good at recognizing it when they see it). True innovation entails anticipating the opportunities for meeting latent need, for solving problems that customers may not even recognize that they have. Prior to the advent of the personal computer—or the Walkman or the warehouse club—no one was asking for it. These were solutions to previously unrecognized problems, answers to as yet unasked questions. But once the answer was available, the question followed quickly.

A customer-centered definition of company mission is in keeping with the tenor of the times. As customers rather than suppliers have the upper hand in a global economy, companies cannot afford to focus inward. All of a company's activities and energies must be focused on and directed to the customer, who is, after all, the source of the company's revenue. Yet despite the "obviousness" and seeming lack of controversy associated with this principle, it is in fact only occasionally acknowledged and even more rarely followed.

There are at least two other contenders for designation as the "First Principle" of business organizations. One of them, in fact, would seem to have already won the title. If you asked most contemporary managers, executives, and economists "Why is a business?" they would most likely answer that the mission of a business is to create *shareholder* value.

This answer is neither irrational nor unreasonable, but it is nonetheless wrong. On one level, it is easy and tempting to see a business as a device that converts invested capital into an income stream, so concern for the shareholders who provide the capital must be central to the enterprise. Regrettably, this concern has not always been in evidence. During the 1960s and 1970s, for example, many executives ran their companies as personal fiefdoms and pursued business strategies primarily designed to boost their own egos and personal incomes. It didn't matter whether the strategy made sense from a business perspective or whether it increased profits or shareholder value. All that mattered was that as their companies grew, the executives' status and compensation soared. Many of these executives came in for a nasty surprise in the takeover wave of the 1980s, but old habits die hard. The cult of shareholder value is a useful corrective to these abuses, but that's all it is.

But an exclusive focus on capital and those who provide it can distract a company from what really counts. I once heard a senior partner of an investment bank open a speech with a very promising sentence. "Every company," he intoned, "is in fundamentally the same business." Right, I said to myself, identifying and meeting customer needs. But he went on to say, "That business is raising and allocating scarce capital." Wrong. Capital is indeed necessary for a company to succeed, just as it needs space for its employees. But generating profits in order to pay for this capital is not the essence of a business, nor is it its mission. It is only one of its requirements. Satisfying shareholders is something that needs to be done, but it is not the reason a company exists.

Stating that a company's mission is to create shareholder value is ultimately useless because it offers no guide for action. It avoids the question, "All right, what do we do now?" Whether you're the CEO, a manager, or an employee on the line, if I tell you that your goal is to create wealth for shareholders, I've told you absolutely nothing useful. If, however, we agree that your mission is to create customer satisfaction, you can actually do something. You can begin by looking around for people who want something (even if they don't know what it is yet) and then find ways to give it to them. In short, creating customer value is a purpose that yields a guide to action. Creating shareholder value yields nothing but questions.

Moreover, creating shareholder value fails as a corporate purpose because, in an important sense, it is demotivating. No one, apart from investment managers, goes to work early because he or she is eager to make shareholders rich. On the other hand, creating customer value—being of service to one's fellow man—enriches one's spirit.

Work seen as service to others rises above mere selfish benefit. Crafting the corporate mission as a call to creating value, serving customers, and changing the world can be a powerful incentive to extraordinary performance and can create strong motivation throughout an organization.

Others would argue that a business enterprise exists to provide employment for its workers. A broader view of the same idea has recently become fashionable. It asserts that a business enterprise exists to answer the needs of all its *stakeholders*—workers, managers, shareholders, customers, suppliers, community, nation, world—of which customers are only one. These are widely held views in Japan and Germany. They are also popular on the American political left.

This viewpoint confuses means with ends. While profit, jobs, and all the rest are desirable and worthy objectives, they cannot be approached directly. The road to all these other destinations lies through customer value.

This first principle starts us on the road to understanding what it takes for a business to succeed, but it isn't enough to get us there. I propose three more.

Principle 2: It is a company's processes that create value for its customers

This principle is, in effect, a restatement of our definition of a process as a group of tasks that create customer value. The tasks are the bits of work that people actually perform, but the tasks themselves do not create value nor do the individuals performing them. It is only whole processes, all the tasks put together, that create value.

Principle 3: Business success comes from superior process performance

This principle follows from the first two: If our purpose is to create value and processes do that, then better processes will do it better. However, this principle also runs counter to the beliefs of most managers. Many believe, for example, that the way to success lies through superior products and/or services. Others believe that it lies through "people," by which they mean a superior workforce. A third group believes that superior strategy is the royal road to success. Let's consider these one at a time.

However superior your products and services may be, the sad fact is that today's changing market conditions guarantee that they won't remain superior for long. A better product might propel a company to success today, but continued success demands that the company have a better product tomorrow and another the day after. From where will this stream of new products come? From processes. Delivering consistently superior products over long periods of time requires a set of consistently superior processes—for product development, manufacturing, order fulfillment, service, etc. It is not any one product but its process capability that gives a company its crucial advantage.

What about a superior workforce? The truth is that even superior people cannot compensate for the deficiencies of inferior processes. A company that bases its success on personal performance, even a small company, is digging its own grave. There are two kinds of individuals that companies can come to depend on. One is the Hero, the other is the Star, and they are both hollow reeds.

The Hero is someone who performs great deeds to overcome defective processes; the Star is an individual of extraordinary talent and ability. A company full of Heroes and Stars will not necessarily be successful, just as all-star teams do not always perform particularly well. On the contrary, the presence of Heroes is a sign of defective processes, whereas the reliance on Stars betrays a lack of appreciation of processes and their importance.

I often meet Heroes when I visit companies. Joe is introduced as someone who saved a key customer's order when it got tied up in the credit department and the customer threatened to cancel. Joe, it seems, stepped in, straightened out the credit department, took the order to the warehouse, had it loaded into a truck, and delivered it himself. "What a Hero!" the manager says, beaming proudly at Joe. But Joe's exploits are an indictment of the company. A Hero is someone who compensates for and overcomes the deficiencies of processes. Well-designed, smoothly operating, and carefully managed processes do not need Heroes. Only bad ones do. By overcoming the flaws in a process, heroics mask serious problems. In the long run a company is far better off improving its processes than looking for Heroes to hire. Heroes come and go, but a good process, like a thing of beauty, is a joy forever.

Similarly, relying on Stars asks for trouble because even marvelously performed tasks cannot overcome the inadequacies of a poorly conceived process. The credit checker, the inventory allocator, the picker, the packer, and the shipper may each do their tasks efficiently, or even brilliantly, but the whole process may still perform poorly. If the process design is replete with handoffs, reviews, checks, and other non-value-adding activities then the process will be slow, inflexible, and error-prone despite the talent and brilliance of the individual workers. Good people working in a great process design will always beat great people struggling with a poor process design.

What about superior company strategy as the basis of success, winning by picking the right businesses for the company to pursue? Unfortunately, as important as strategy can be to a company's success, a strategic plan without the processes to implement it is just talk, a pile of useless (albeit brilliant) documents. Moreover, strategies have increasingly become virtual commodities, easily disseminated and imitated. Execution—process—is the key to contemporary success, not plans—strategies.

Principle 4: Superior process performance is achieved by having a superior process design, the right people to perform it, and the right environment for them to work in

First, design. The structure, layout, and organization of the process—how the individual tasks are performed and integrated—is a critical determinant of how well the process performs. A process design full of handoffs cannot be fast or accurate; a process with redundancies cannot be inexpensive; a process entailing endless reviews cannot be flexible. A process cannot perform better than its design allows. It is perhaps most accurate to say that the process design defines the limits of process performance—how well it can possibly perform if all performers do what is expected of them.

Next, people. In order to compete in a world of changing customer preferences and rapidly evolving technologies, many companies have adopted a product development process known as concurrent engineering. This process brings groups of people with different skills—such as manufacturing, engineering, finance, and marketing—to work together. They seek to develop new products in a manner that ensures not only that all aspects of the new product work but that they work together.

But no matter how well designed this product development process may be, it needs the right people to implement it. It needs engineers who will listen to and respect the views of marketers, marketing experts who understand enough technology to grasp the engineers' concerns, and manufacturing specialists capable of translating customer needs into their operational implications. Without such people, the best designed product development process will not develop great products.

Note that the *right* people does not necessarily mean the best, or even superior, people. Who is better, an engineer who has top technical expertise but lacks team skills or an adequate technician with terrific team skills? The answer depends on the design of the process in which the engineer will be asked to work. Some processes need the technical expert; others, the team player. Superior process performance needs superior design and people well-matched to the design. This provides a reprieve from the daunting goal of having the "best" people that many companies set themselves. That would take winning the lottery. Having the right people just requires focus and discipline.

Last, environment. Even the right people working with a superior process design won't deliver superior performance unless they care deeply about what they're doing. Without motivation, the process design will remain a piece of paper, and people's abilities will be mere credentials on a résumé. Unmotivated people merely go through the motions. Organizations must have a spirit and a soul to encourage people to exercise their potential and to make a process hum.

From where does such motivation come? It is the result not of any one factor—an executive's speech, the attitudes of peers, or the company's measurement and reward system—but of a great many factors that together I call the *environment* of the organization. The environment shapes people's attitudes and feelings. The right environment will encourage, motivate, and liberate people to perform. The wrong one discourages and demotivates.

To summarize our principles:

- The purpose of a company is to create customer value
- Customer value is created through processes
- Business success results from superior processes performance
- Superior process performance is achieved by having:
  - superior process design
  - the right people
  - the right environment

Business success is not mysterious; it has very concrete and specific prerequisites. But neither is it automatic. To implement our prescription for business success requires that we rethink the role of management.

The traditional definition of management has focused on control and decision-making activities. But more broadly, management's real mission is to assemble the ingredients needed for organizational success. That means that management must design and implement superior processes and monitor them to ensure their ongoing health. Management must determine the kinds of people these processes require, find sources for them, get them into the company, and ensure that they acquire and maintain the skills they need. Management must fashion an environment that will instill and reinforce the behaviors and attitudes that people must exhibit in order for the processes to work. After that, it is management's job to get out of the way and let the people perform their processes.

Corporate success is no more the product of management heroics than of worker heroics. Carefully crafted and measured processes, carefully chosen and nurtured people, and a carefully created and tended environment will yield success without other forms of management intervention. These three fundamental management responsibilities can, in fact, be associated with three specific management roles.

The architect Louis Sullivan said that form follows function. In the process-centered world that could be amended to say that *role* follows function. The first managerial role is that of process owner, an individual responsible for ensuring that we have a high performance process. The second is the coach, someone concerned with providing the organization with the people the processes will require. The third is the leader, an individual charged with designing and shaping the overall environment in which everything else takes place.

With this framework and a relatively precise definition of

the requirements of business and management we can move on to explore how it all plays out. What better place to observe it than on an actual playing field, where process teams of highly motivated individuals clash on hard ground to the cheers and groans of paying customers?

CHAPTER 7

WHAT'S FOOTBALL GOT TO DO WITH IT?

GAME THEORY is a branch of mathematics used to model and analyze competitive behavior. I'd like to propose a little game theory of my own, namely that the best way to see the theory of the process-centered corporation in action is by watching an American professional football game. This is not another tiresome homily on how sports is a metaphor for business or for life in general. Rather, it says that a football team is in fact a process-centered organization and that we have much to learn from its management structure.

In his seminal 1988 *Harvard Business Review* article "The Coming of the New Organization," Peter Drucker suggested that the appropriate model for the modern organization is the symphony orchestra: a collection of highly trained specialists working in close rapport under a conductor's overall leadership. As usual, Drucker found an elegant and insightful metaphor, but it's lacking in some critical dimensions.

An orchestra executes a plan—performing the score of a musical work—under conditions that are static and unlikely to change: the score will not be rewritten in the midst of the performance; it is unlikely that the second bassoonist will suddenly have to cover for an incapacitated first-chair cellist; the orchestra pit will not become engulfed in flames. Moreover, the orchestra members, while skilled musicians, operate under the strict discipline of the conductor. They proceed at his tempo, follow his interpretation, play and stop when he indicates. Finally, each individual is a narrowly focused specialist; the conductor is responsible for the overall outcome. An orchestra may be an ensemble, but it would be a stretch to call it a team.

A better model is the contemporary football team. Football is played in a constant state of flux, much like business. A corporate strategy resembles a game plan much more than it does a musical score. Moreover, a football team's organization and management structure bear an uncanny resemblance to those of a process-centered company. So it's worth our while to spend some time examining the roles and relationships on a football team. We can explore some new concepts while staying on familiar turf.

We should begin by noting that a football team engages in two major processes: offense and defense. Each of these processes is a collection of tasks that together achieve a result. In the offense process the tasks include blocking, running, passing, catching, huddling, hiking, and setting up on the line. Alone, none of them accomplishes anything, but when they are combined by an overall choreography—the design of the play (process)—yards are gained and points scored. The individuals who perform the process constitute a team, both in name and in fact. Well-thrown blocks without powerful running or brilliant passes without reliable receiving achieve nothing. The only aim (for the offense) is crossing the goal line (with intermediate indicators of yards gained and time of possession).

The football team has two individuals who are responsible for its processes and who play the role of process owner; these are the offensive coordinator and the defensive coordinator. What does the coordinator do for the team? To begin with, he *designs* the process. Offensive and defensive patterns do not establish themselves on their own; the choreography of offensive plays is especially intricate. The offensive coordinator conceives and designs the plays. He specifies the order of the tasks, who is to perform them, and how they fit together—in short, he scripts what we would call the process design.

Once on the field, however, the teams are largely self-directed. When issues occur as plays unfold, running backs don't dash to the sideline to get the offensive coordinator's opinion about whether to sweep around the end on a play designed to go off tackle, nor do wide receivers seek approval for cutting right instead of left because the defensive cornerback has committed himself. The offensive team's job is to follow the given design as best they can, adapting it to the very rapidly changing realities of their situation. While the offensive coordinator—the process owner—may be the designer, he never takes the field. The players are the implementors.

In addition to designing the plays, the offensive coordinator brings them to life. The coordinator fields the team, selecting from the available personnel the ones best suited to the rigors of the particular design. He familiarizes them with the play and trains them in its execution. Should players have questions or concerns about it, they turn to him. The offensive coordinator also typically calls the play, deciding which design is best for a particular circumstance.

The coordinator's duties don't end there. He also has the ongoing responsibility to improve his plays. The coordinator is constantly seeking ways to enhance the effectiveness of the offense, seeing how well different plays work against specific defensive alignments and modifying them—sometimes during the game—in order to make them perform better.

In short, the offensive coordinator is the individual responsible for bringing together all the disparate elements of the offense into a coherent process. The very word "coordinator" is evocative; the real work is done by the players, whose only need for a "manager" is to coordinate them and their work.

While the coordinator provides the play, another important member of the management team provides something equally essential: the players who will perform it. The offensive team, for example, needs a variety of talents. Huge men adept at blocking form the offensive line. Wide receivers must be speedsters with incredible hand-eye coordination. Offensive backs have great peripheral vision and fast reflexes, and can run like hell. The quarterback and his backups must be expert in reading defenses, passing, scrambling, and running. It is the "position coaches" who make sure that these talents are available.

A position coach's role is very different from the coordinator's. His mission is to train and develop the athletes who will perform the specific tasks required by the coordinator. The line coach helps his charges develop the ability to block low, pull for a running back, and fool the defense into jumping offsides. Other position coaches perform similar services for other team members.

Position coaches are teachers, but they must also be more than that. The position coach is a player's counselor and mentor as well. While the coordinator monitors the plays, the coach monitors the players. He observes their performance and provides them with feedback and advice. The position coach is also responsible for finding, acquiring, and maintaining the talent pool the team will need. He scouts the prospects and selects the ones who possess the skills he is looking for. At the other end of their careers, he advises the old pros when it's time to pack it in.

All these diverse activities have a common theme: ensuring not only that the team has the players with the needed skills but that those players are mentally and physically prepared to play. Each position coach's job is to manage and develop a specific part of the team's human resources. Position coaches are the providers, and process owners the deployers, of the team's human resources.

This distinction between concerns for people and concerns for process lies at the heart of the process-centered organization. The members of a company's product development process team, for example, are likely to represent a wide variety of skills and disciplines: marketing, engineering, manufacturing, procurement. As process team members, their common concern is the performance of the process, the striving for a score. As individuals, however, they have divergent backgrounds, interests, and futures. They are unlikely to remain members of a particular product development process team forever—or even to work on product development at all. Therefore, they need to develop their own skills and prepare for futures independent of the process. In football each player wants to execute each play as well as possible, but is also concerned about his career as a whole. The same is true in business.

There's one more essential member of a football staff: the head coach. What does the head coach do? The offensive and defensive coordinators are designing and calling the plays; the position coaches are finding and training the players. What's left to the head coach is to be the team's *leader*. He's the one who names the coordinators and the coaches, motivates the players, and creates an environment for success.

In his first year as head coach of the Minnesota Vikings, Dennis Green described to an interviewer his role during a game: "The offensive coordinator will come to me and say, 'It's fourth and one. We're going for it.' And I'll say, 'Okay.' Then I get on the phone and call the defensive coordinator and say, 'Get ready.' Then I pray." Asked what he missed most in his role as head coach, Green replied, "Coaching."

The head coach's role goes beyond the narrow concerns of plays and players. He develops and integrates the team as a whole. He fashions the game plan—in business parlance, the strategic direction. He manages, or coaches, the coordinators and coaches. And he instills in all team members an esprit de corps, both through his everyday actions and with halftime pep talks. Dennis Green said his most important contribution to the team was in coaching the second string at practice sessions. That way, he said, "I show that there's no such thing as an unimportant job in this organization." Instilling the right attitudes in his players can mean the difference between lackluster and extraordinary performance.

The coordinators create plays; the coaches create players; the head coach creates an organization. He is one part strategist, one part motivator, and one part integrator.

The importance of the head coach is witnessed by franchises that continue to be successful despite many changes in personnel. The continuing presence of the head coach is responsible for this success. It is similarly demonstrated when the performance of a team with the same players and coordinators takes a dramatic turn following the appointment of a new head coach. Especially in modern professional sports, players' abilities do not differ widely except for a handful of extraordinarily talented atheletes. All are extremely skilled. As pro players themselves testify, competition at their rarefied level is largely an exercise in mental preparedness and concentration. Attitude is what motivates people to peak performance. The inspiration and encouragement that the head coach engenders are critical to the team's success.

This is the head coach's most important contribution: to create the values and cultural context that guide and shape what everyone else does. In the constant movement of football the players cannot be closely supervised—things move too fast. Even trying to control them creates the wrong feelings and attitudes. People can't be moved to high performance by policing, but only by instilling in them the drive to do it on their own. Dwight Eisenhower defined leadership as the art of getting people to do things because they want to.

In professional football the head coach weaves together the offensive and defensive processes, allocates resources, and sets strategy. The head coach, however, is *not* a traditional boss sitting at the top and exercising command. He's literally and figuratively on the sidelines. Key decisions are made close to the action so that flexibility and responsiveness are maximized. The quarterback on the field is free to call an audible when the situation warrants it.

In business, too, someone must weave everything together. In a company that produces goods someone must make sure that product development and order fulfillment *integrate*, not merely coexist. Someone must ensure that the investments in order fulfillment and product development make sense. Someone must set the overall strategy. Someone must motivate everyone to perform at his or her very best. That someone is the executive leader. But, like the head coach, he's not on the field. Senior executives don't design and make products, fill orders, or answer customer questions. The performers on the front line do the work that needs to be done. The leader creates the context in which they do it.

To summarize, the modern football team is an almost perfect model for the organization and structure of the process-centered enterprise. Football teams perform two major processes that are executed by players with diverse skills working together toward a common objective. Each process is guided by a coordinator whose role is similar to that of a process owner. Meanwhile, position coaches nurture and develop the players so that they can execute coordinators' plays. The head coach motivates and supports them. These correspond to the three primary roles that business managers fill in process-centered organizations.

Now it's time to leave the comparatively placid world of the gridiron and return to the hurly-burly of the business world. But the parallels between the two will remain long after the fourth quarter is over.

CHAPTER 8

THE END OF THE ORGANIZATIONAL CHART

IN TRADITIONAL businesses a manager has responsibility both for the work that has to be done and for the workers who are to do it. It would be inconceivable in a conventional organization for the management of the work and of the workers to be split. But in a process-centered organization that's exactly what happens. The process—the coordinated tasks that create value for the customer—is ultimately the responsibility of the process owner, as we have seen. The performers, the professionals who come together to carry out the process, are the responsibility of a coach.

In traditional organizations department managers hired and developed the talent needed to perform the work of their departments, but in process-centered organizations there aren't any department managers (or departments for that matter). There are process owners who make sure that processes are organized in efficient and productive ways, but, like the coordinators on a football team, they are focused on process, not personnel. So a company is left with the same questions as is a football team: How do you ensure the development and maintenance of the required skills in each discipline? How do you nurture and support the individual workers so as to get the most out of them? Who is going to look out for the company's future by hiring the talent and developing the skills that will be needed to keep it running successfully over the long haul?

Enter the coach. Like their counterparts in football, corporate coaches are needed to maintain the skills and develop the talent in each area of expertise that the company requires. This means that there will be coaches for engineers, others for sales representatives, more for information systems developers, and so on through the company's equivalents of quarterbacks, linemen, and wide receivers.

The term "coach" has many pleasant connotations. But the job of a coach isn't just to make going to work more appealing for the workers. The role of the coach is critical to an organization's success. No matter how well designed a process is, it's the people who make it work. As Marv Levy, head coach of the Buffalo Bills, has said, "Game plans don't win football games. Players do." "The only thing that distinguishes us is our people and what's in their heads and hearts," says Richard Chandler, CEO of Sunrise Medical of Torrance, California. "Your most important investment is anything that educates them and puts more in their heads or gives more motivation in their hearts." The coach is responsible for what is in people's heads.

In the long run the quality of an organization's coaching is a key determinant of whether it succeeds or fails. Process design alone is not enough. As more companies learn how to create state-of-the-art processes, the advantage will belong to those with an institutionalized capacity for staffing these processes with well-selected and well-trained people. That is the coach's mission.

A coach is also the performer of a process: hiring and developing people. This includes both finding capable new employees and making existing employees more capable. Every process has a customer, and in this case the coach's customers are the owners of the other processes that need qualified people. Thus, the engineering coach's customers include the product development process owner, the customer service process owner, and the owners of all other processes that need engineers. Although the coach's process produces no direct value for external customers, it produces a great deal of indirect value. The coach's product is personnel who perform all the other processes of the company.

The biggest lie in contemporary American business is one proudly proclaimed by many executives: "Our people are our most important resource." They often say it, but their actions belie their words, for the truth is that in most companies no one really looks after the "people." So-called human resource departments are too often staffed by functionaries responsible only for implementing bureaucratic procedures and ensuring regulatory compliance.

But a coach is not just another functionary. The true role of the coach is to develop human resources. Because it is in both their interests, coaches and employees work together to devise career development plans. This helps the workers to end up where they want to be and the company to have the talent and skills it needs. These plans consider such questions as: What mix of different processes should the employee work on over time in order to develop the best understanding of the company? What additional training does the employee need to keep up with developments in his or her field? What are the employee's weaknesses? How can the employee improve?

The coach must also consider the skills that the company will need in the future. If a coach realizes, for example, that the company's strategic direction will generate a need for engineers who are knowledgeable in high-temperature ceramics then he or she should steer some people in that direction. This works to the benefit of both the individuals who want skills that are going to be valuable and the company that will need these skills.

American Standard is a $5 billion corporation with three main businesses: plumbing products; Trane, the heating and air conditioning manufacturer; and Wabco, a maker of air brakes for trucks and buses. In the late 1980s American Standard successfully fought off an acquisition bid through a leveraged buyout. As a result the company ended up with so much debt that the profits generated by its existing modes of operation wouldn't even pay the interest. Out of necessity the company embarked on a program of reengineering that has yielded astonishing results. Under the leadership of CEO Emmanuel Kampouris, American Standard has focused on speed of operation as its key goal. By reducing cycle times for order fulfillment and related processes, inventory turns have tripled across the company, inventory savings have exceeded half a billion dollars, and the need for working capital has been virtually eliminated. There are parts of American Standard today with *negative* working capital requirements.

In order to hold and extend the gains achieved by this effort, American Standard has organized all parts of the company around processes and has embarked on a major effort to provide every individual in the company with a coach. The following is a paraphrase of American Standard's job description for a coach:

- Assess the present and future demand for workers with particular skills. By working with process owners and general managers, the coaches determine what kinds of people and how many of them will be needed to staff the processes.

- Develop the supply of skilled individuals. The coach formulates a hiring strategy, a training program, and other steps to ensure that the supply of people matches the demand.
- Allocate resources. The coach acts as a broker, matching people with process owners' needs. In doing this the coach must balance the immediate needs of the process against the longer-term developmental requirements of the individual.
- Guide and mentor employees. The coach is the individual to whom an employee will turn for personal and professional counseling, as well as for feedback and career guidance.
- Intervene to help resolve performance problems. When an employee experiences difficulties on an assignment, the coach will act as an honest facilitator, balancing the perspectives of the employee, teammates, and the process owner in order to find a solution to the problem.

At American Standard the coach plays the vital role of ensuring that processes are equipped with the people they need. American Standard is in the vanguard of this movement, for while the term "coach" has been much bandied about in recent years, it is in fact quite hard to find people who are actually functioning as coaches (as opposed to merely having the title). This is in part because teaching and counseling are not things that traditional managers have generally valued or done well. But in process-centered companies the work of the coach is essential. If processes are going to work smoothly and efficiently, you must have able and available workers, and that requires effective coaches.

What kind of people make good coaches? A process owner is a kind of entrepreneur running a mini-business. The coach, in contrast, is primarily a "people" person. The coach must have a keen understanding of the company's business and of his or her discipline; without these, the coach won't be able to evaluate the workers' skills and the company's needs. But the coach doesn't need to have the very best skills in his or her discipline. In fact, the people on the front line should be the ones with the best skills in their disciplines. The skills that coaches need most are those associated with developing other people's skills: teaching, listening, evaluating, advising. A great football player doesn't necessarily make a great coach, and many great coaches have had undistinguished playing careers.

Players can afford to have large egos, but coaches can't. They must be good at sublimating their own needs. Their gratification comes from the attainment of others, a vicarious form of success.

The guard who throws the key block for the touchdown play is cheered, the wide receiver who catches the pass is hoisted on his teammates' shoulders, the quarterback leaves the field to roars—whereas a bucket of Gatorade on ice douses the coach. If there's glory on the sidelines, it's not the showy sort. But the game is won there every bit as much as on the field.

Someone recently asked me how to prevent coaching from becoming "women's work." This was not a sexist question—although the phrase "women's work" is—but rather a display of real insight. Traditional organizations have thought of helping as women's work, and it has rarely paid well. This cannot be the case in a successful process-centered company. Coaching is a job for the wise and highly respected of either gender. A single individual, no matter how talented or knowledgeable, can accomplish only so much. A teacher, however, multiplies the impact of his or her knowledge by sharing it with others. To recognize the crucial importance of the coach's role, companies must reward them appropriately. They must also ensure the development of coaching itself as a real skill and profession by providing coaches with a coach of their own. Coaches educate and develop; they truly are a most important resource.

We have established what coaches do; we must now ask with whom they do it. There's a small problem here: No handy collective noun exists for the category of people that a coach coaches. It's not a team. Teams are what the process owner guides. It's certainly not a department, a relic of the old regime. We'll call it a center of excellence.

By center of excellence I mean the people in the organization who possess a particular skill or profession. A typical business might have centers of excellence in such areas as sales, engineering, marketing, and finance. Clearly, these centers will vary across companies. A football team has centers of excellence in blocking, quarterbacking, and tackling; a pharmaceutical firm is likely to have them in physician relations, biochemistry, and manufacturing (among others).

Process-centering takes the old functional department of the traditional organization and deconstructs it into two mechanisms: the process team, where work is done, and the center of excellence, where skills are enhanced and people are developed. The center of excellence can be thought of as a talent pool or a skill bank from which process team members are drawn. Its ultimate responsibility is to ensure that a company has the best possible human assets and makes the best possible use of them.

A center of excellence is *not* a place where work is done. That happens in the process teams: product development by a product development team, order fulfillment by an order fulfillment team, and so on. Rather, the company's personnel are trained, developed, and mentored by means of its centers of excellence: engineers via the engineering center, financial experts via the financial center. However, the centers are not simply the old functional departments renamed. They are their vestiges, what is left of the departments after the work has been removed (and put into the process teams).

This distinction must be stressed. The old engineering department produced engineering drawings; the engineering center of excellence produces engineers—who create their drawings and do their other work in process teams.

What do terms like "sales representative," "finance expert," and "engineer" mean in a process-centered context? Traditionally, an engineer was someone who worked in the engineering department and a finance expert was someone who hung his hat in finance. But when these functional departments are replaced by process teams as the basic unit of the organization, what does it mean to be an engineer?

Fundamentally, I submit, sales, engineering, and the like represent *skills* critical to the success of the organization. A sales representative is not someone who works in the sales department. A sales representative is someone skilled at sales, who may be working in any of a number of different processes. The sales center of excellence consists of all the people in the organization with these sales skills, and so a sales representative is someone who is a member of the sales center of excellence. The center of excellence is the mechanism for ensuring that the caliber of these skills is maintained and enhanced. A coach (or more than one if the center has many members) will be assigned to a center of excellence to develop its members and ensure that their skills are up to snuff.

Companies usually start with centers of excellence based on their traditional departments—sales, engineering, finance. In time, however, many companies find new definitions and names that are both more elastic and more precise for their centers. "Sales" is actually too limited to convey the professional abilities underlying that activity. Certainly sales representatives must speak their customers' language, be able to identify with their concerns, and represent their needs. But others—including many marketing professionals and customer service representatives—need the same set of talents and skills, which is why it may be better to have a center of excellence for "customer interaction" rather than for "sales." Similarly, a "technical design" center of excellence may be more relevant than one for just "engineering."

Centers of excellence may be thought of as in-house versions of professional associations, such as the American Medical Association for physicians or the American Bar Association for lawyers. Such professional societies serve a number of functions. They offer ongoing education programs, help members keep up with the latest developments in the field, and provide opportunities for networking and experience sharing. The center of excellence offers analogous services. It provides its members with the training they require to maintain and upgrade their skills; it serves as a gateway or point of entry into the firm for new techniques, tools, and technologies; and it offers a forum for sharing experiences and war stories. One of the most crucial things a center of excellence does is provide a channel of communication so that people can share their expertise and learn from one another. A traffic manager in Dallas may have a good experience with a new truck leasing firm, so he will share it with his colleagues in his center (wherever they are physically located). A finance specialist in San Diego finds serious glitches in a new computer program and warns colleagues around the country. Clearly, modern communications technology is the glue that holds these virtual organizations together.

A center of excellence may be divided into smaller groups of people with a very narrow common concern. Chrysler conducts new product development with process teams called "platform teams," in which the traditional disciplines of engineering, marketing, and the rest function as centers of excellence (called "clubs"). They have gone so far as to create a "wiper club" comprising the engineers on all platform teams who are concerned with windshield wipers. This enables them to share information and experience and to learn from each other.

Although their forms are many, centers of excellence are alike in their task and function—to "leverage our talent," as expressed by Craig Goldman, Chase Manhattan Bank's chief information officer. The centers of excellence in Chase's information systems arena are defined in terms of particular areas of technology. Members who have jobs in every location and business unit throughout the world assemble quarterly to discuss new programs and establish timetables and standards for evaluating new technology within their arenas. They are also linked electronically to form a "global community" that shares information, especially about new products. Thus a problem in Singapore can be posted on a computer bulletin or dialog board and a member elsewhere can reply with an already devised solution. "I know exactly how to fix that because I broke my legs on it three years ago. Here's what to do."

If you're touring an office or plant and ask to see a center of excellence, don't expect to be led to a room with mahogany panels and a control board modeled on the Starship *Enterprise*. There may be no room at all; centers of excellence are often virtual organizations with only a minimal physical presence. If you press the engineering coach to show you the engineering center of excellence, he or she might show you a training facility or might produce a group photograph of all the company's engineers, probably snapped at the annual engineering picnic. A more sophisticated response would be to show you the electronic mail distribution list that is used to interconnect all the engineers. The collection of people, together with the mechanism that binds them together, in fact constitutes the center of excellence.

If we attempt to visualize the organization we have been describing, we see independent process teams operating largely on their own, but with the guidance of a process owner and the support of coaches. Figure 3 expresses this image. This is definitely *not* your typical organizational chart. In fact, it is not an organizational chart at all. You will search

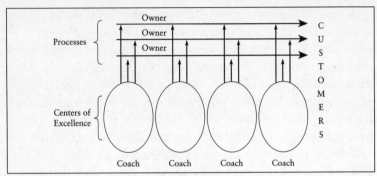

Figure 3

in vain for indicators of hierarchy, power, and authority. Instead, it shows how resources come together to produce value; it depicts the business, not its administration.

Arrayed at top are the company's processes, each with its owner, directed toward producing customer value. The ovals are the centers of excellence, the incubators where people are developed and continually renewed. The vertical arrows represent the deployment of people from centers of excellence to the process teams.

Two questions invariably strike people when they see this picture and try to imagine how their own organization might embody it. The first is: Where do I fit in? The second is related: Who's my boss?

We touched on these questions in chapters 3 and 4 when we saw how workers are becoming professionals and how titles and compensation are rethought in a process-centered company. We'll approach these questions again, but now from a structural standpoint. The real question is: Who's in charge of whom here?

Let's say you've just joined the company after graduating from engineering school. When you arrive, your name is registered at the engineering center of excellence. After all, engineering is your profession and you need a professional identity. When you are assigned to work on a process, your name will be noted on that process as well (or in multiple processes if you're dividing your time). Thus your name is entered in two, maybe more, places on our business diagram.

On the process team's roster, your name is written in pencil because the assignment is probably—in fact, almost certainly—not a permanent one. In time you'll be asked to work on a different process, if for no other reason than to broaden your perspective and knowledge.

In the center of excellence, however, your membership will probably be permanent, so your name is written in ink. As an engineer you will move among many processes during your career. You might work on product development, order acquisition, or order fulfillment—any process that needs an engineer. Throughout, however, you will remain an engineer. A few people may switch professions. A customer service specialist could acquire the skills to become a finance person or even an engineer. In these cases they would move from one center of excellence to another. But these transitions would not be matters of simple retraining. They mean acquiring a new profession, and so would require a new professional education—and possibly even a return to school to get it. There is a world of difference between an engineer moving to the order acquisition process and the same engineer becoming a salesperson. One is a change of job; the other is a change of career. For most people, it's likely to be one profession and one center of excellence.

So, if your name is written in several places, for whom do you work? Who is your boss? In a process-centered organization there are five possible answers to that question, but none of them is the right one.

Perhaps the first and most obvious nominee for the boss's title is the process owner. He or she defines your work and specifies how it should be carried out. You may have considerable latitude in execution, but at the end of the day he or she designs the process, calls the shots, and sets your agenda.

Your coach is also something of a boss. He or she is responsible for hiring and firing you and for training and developing you. Counseling, raises, and pink slips are all delivered by your coach.

When it comes to making operating decisions, you are your own boss. Professionals don't scurry to a supervisor to resolve every issue. They handle most problems themselves.

At the same time, you could say that your teammates are your bosses because their evaluations of you and your performance are the most important. They're the closest to you; they know when you're performing well and have a vested interest in informing you when you're not.

Finally, you could reply that the customer who ultimately pays your salary is your boss. In the sense of setting your priorities and determining where you should be directing your energy, the customer definitely has the most clout. In this era of increasing choice and competition it is a big mistake to ignore this *capo di tutti capi*, this boss of all bosses.

In fact, in a process-centered organization none of these five nominees is the real boss because the very concept of boss itself disappears. A "boss" is a creature of the pyramid: a single person who stands above you, telling you what to do and how to do it. In a process-centered environment the role disappears. More precisely, it is dispersed among many people, none of whom can accurately be called your boss.

Some die-hard organizational chartists will insist that the diagram on page 126 is only a restatement of the notorious matrix management. In matrix management people have multiple (usually two) bosses, with one indicated by a solid line to indicate primary authority and the other by a dotted line to show secondary authority. Thus an engineer might simultaneously report to the head of engineering and to a particular product manager or the head of a geographical region. Designed to achieve a multidimensional perspective, matrix management instead often created organizational chaos. Each of the bosses had a different agenda, leaving the employee with incongruent goals and a bad case of cognitive dissonance. "If my boss calls, get his name" is a refrain frequently heard in companies operating under matrix management.

Our diagram is not that of a matrix organization with two bosses. Our diagram is one with no bosses at all. It displays no conventional lines of authority. To return to football, imagine asking an offensive guard if he "reports" to the offensive coordinator or the line coach. The question is foolish. It would be more accurate to say that they both support him: one by providing plays, the other by training him. Similarly, the process owner and the coach are not bosses but people with specific assignments: one to design and improve process, the other to offer development and advice. Ultimately the responsibility for achieving results lies with the individual professional. Both the process owner and the coach are supporting resources to help the individual accomplish that goal, not controllers with their own agendas. Moira Lardakis is president of Progressive Insurance's Ohio division. When asked if the performers of the claims process in Ohio report to her or to the process owner of claims, she replies, "'Reports to' doesn't mean much around here." This Zen-like response conveys the essence of the process-centered organization.

Not only does the quality of management change in a process-centered company, but so does its quantity. As we've said, it is the rare multibillion-dollar enterprise that has more than one hundred processes and subprocesses—which means not many process-owner chairs are waiting to be filled. Process owners will have assistants and supporting staff, but the real managerial responsibility for processes does not require large numbers of personnel.

How many coaches will there be? The old managerial supervisor ratio—the number of people a typical traditional manager could control—normally ranged between seven to one and ten to one. But coaches enable and support; they don't supervise and control. Organizations making the transition to process centering typically assign twenty to twenty-five employees to each coach and find, remarkably, that this number steadily increases over time. As coaches develop their own skills—and even more important, as professionals learn how to be coached and how to operate autonomously—the ratio often increases to fifty and even sixty "protégés" for each coach.

Simple arithmetic, therefore, suggests a probable reduction of over 50 percent in the number of people with "managerial" job titles. Whole layers of supervisors, directors, and vice presidents will be replaced by a relative handful of process owners and coaches. This, of course, is already happening. Progressive Insurance's focus on process has largely eliminated the need for traditional management. COO Bruce Marlow believes the company can double its revenue without adding a single manager. In 1995 UPS reduced its management ranks by 5,000. At some Federal-Mogul plants there are ninety factory workers for each foreman. Most of AT&T's 40,000 layoffs announced in 1996 are of managers.

What will then become of today's management cadres? Some will no doubt transform themselves into process owners or coaches, although this transition will be harder than many anticipate. Most of what managers have learned from advancing themselves in a traditional structure is at best useless and at worst dysfunctional for the new environment. Very few have the disciplined process design and improvement skills required for process ownership. Even fewer are comfortable with personal coaching after years in a corporate culture that put a premium on ambition, aggression, and personal toughness. Many old-style managers won't want to make the transition—not because the transition itself is so tough, but because the new work is. One insightful executive who *has* adapted speaks of "a trick" having been played on managers. One reason many of them worked hard when they were young, he explains, was to get to a senior level where they would be able to ease up and enjoy their perks. But the new-style management, which requires a relentless drive for continuous improvement or an intense concern for enhancing people and their abilities, is extraordinarily demanding. The net result of all this is that most companies making the transition to a process orientation find themselves awash in surplus managers—and simultaneously hard-pressed to fill the new roles of coach and process owner.

The greatest difficulty in making the transition comes for those at what we might call the "upper middle" of most organizations. The people who have reached this level generally have been away from substantive work for so long that they have lost touch with it, yet they lack the leadership skills needed to rise to the very top. Many of these people will leave in search of organizations that haven't yet opted for process orientation.

For first-level and lower middle-management men and women, the most commonly traveled route will take them back to the front lines from which they came. This is not as grim as it may sound. After all, they were promoted into management because they had good skills in their disciplines and performed well. They are likely to succeed again when back in a position where they can use them.

Thus a process-centered corporation's best performers will no longer spend their time watching over others. They will again be free to excel—and to look toward financial rewards as promising as those in a managerial career. Corporations must adjust their compensation standards to take account of this phenomenon. Drastically reducing the salary of managers who return to "real" work would send a dangerous message: that value-adding work isn't as important as non-value-adding administration.

The process-centered organization is consequently best thought of as a somewhat loose association of professionals:

performers, process owners, and coaches. It is not a rigid, highly structured hierarchy. Nonetheless, some agency is required to bring all these elements together and make sure they work effectively. This is the role of the business leader, the counterpart of football's head coach.

Without a guiding hand even the most highly capable people can fail to produce the needed results. Processes may be well-designed, but they may be targeted at the wrong markets or at achieving irrelevant objectives; people may be skilled but unfocused and unmotivated; each individual process may be a paragon of performance, but not fit in with any of the others. It is the leader's responsibility to bring all the pieces together and thereby keep the ship on course and moving ahead.

What a leader adds to an organization is strategy, motivation, and integration. First, the leader provides the overall vision for the business. Just as an entrepreneur originates the idea for the product or service that is the core of the company, the business leader must formulate and communicate a picture of the company that everyone can understand and contribute to. The process owners cannot shape their processes, the coaches cannot develop their people, and the performers cannot perform their work without a sense of the purpose of the enterprise. Who are our customers and what problems of theirs do we propose to solve? That is the basic identity question facing any company, and it is the business leader's job to answer it.

This question cannot be answered once and for all, or even once a decade. With continuing technological and social change, the very definition of a company must be subject to regular scrutiny. How long could a company continue to define itself as a minicomputer manufacturer with the advent of the PC? What does it mean to be a publisher in the age of the CD-ROM, or a television network when the home set receives five hundred channels? What is the future for branded consumer goods in a world of generics? These are the most fundamental and perplexing business questions of all, and they cannot be answered in a formulaic fashion. These are not the structured decisions so beloved by the traditional business school. They take real appreciation of the customer, an understanding of technology and its direction, imagination, creativity, and ultimately a deep belief in one's own judgment. In chapter 12 we will offer some tools to help leaders grapple with these questions, but they are only tools. There is no substitute for the leader's personal insight and foresight.

In addition to shaping the firm's vision (or strategy, to use a much overused term), the leader must also shape the thinking and attitudes of the people in the organization. This is the charismatic side of leadership, in which the leader touches the emotional side of people to bring out their very best. Exceptional personal performance is rarely a purely logical act. Most people do not do their very best simply for monetary reward. They must be inspired by a transcendent vision of the meaning of their work.

Through personal example, direct interaction, and endless communications the leader fosters the attitudes and spirit that a high-performance organization requires. Reduced to short phrases, the messages can sound simplistic and clichéd: your work matters; we are all on the same team; the customer pays our salaries. But brought to life by a true leader, they are uplifting and inspirational. There is no substitute for sincerity; simply mouthing politically correct platitudes does not make for inspiration or leadership. The true leader must express his or her own inner visions and beliefs, not simply cite the conventional wisdom. This aspect of leadership is not one that is part of traditional management development programs. It has little to do with financial analysis and everything to do with character.

A remark by Ross Perot can help us understand this dimension of leadership. Asked by an interviewer if General Colin Powell would make a good president of the United States,

Perot replied that Colin Powell would make a great president of the United States and a great president of any corporation. The second half of this statement might give one pause. Why should an army general, no matter how effective in that role, be expected to do well heading a chemical company or an insurance firm?

Think back to the Gulf War. That war—like a business—was not won because of the caliber of its ammunition, but because of the caliber of its processes. The two critical ones were the offensive process that devastated the Iraqi military and the logistics process that got a mind-boggling quantity of personnel and materiel to the theater of operations in record time. Generals Norman Schwarzkopf and Gus Pagonis, not Colin Powell, were the process owners—the designers and shapers—of these two processes. Powell's contribution was more subtle but just as vital. What were your reactions when General Powell came on television to discuss the war effort? How did you *feel*? If you were like most Americans, civilian or military, you felt uplifted. You felt inspired, confident, and trusting. You believed in Colin Powell, you believed what he said, and you were ready to do your part. The courage displayed by the American soldiers in the Gulf could not be imposed from the outside; it could only be brought out by a leader who reached inside.

The third contribution that the leader makes to the organization is knitting together its processes so that they succeed not only individually but collectively. To that end, the leader sets the agenda for the process owners and coaches, allocating the organization's resources in a way that will achieve the best results for the enterprise as a whole. The leader intervenes as necessary to ensure that the various processes fit together so that the output of one process can become the input of another. The leader also serves as a coach to the process owners and coaches. After all, they need support and counseling too. The leader is also the owner of the "management process," the process of designing processes and improving and developing personnel. Someone has to decide how the company will be run—the leader doesn't perform the running personally, but does shape how others do.

We have been using the term "business leader." Some companies are using more conventional terms like "general manager" for this role, while others are employing more daring and evocative names like "business *owner*." The latter is particularly suggestive and helpful. In a large organization the business leader plays the role of the small enterprise's entrepreneur/owner.

It won't be much easier for the typical executive to become a business leader than for his or her middle-management counterparts to become coaches and process owners. The hardest part of this transition is likely to be the adjustment in personal style that it requires. An executive is a decision maker and an order giver. The rest of the organization exists to carry out his or her wishes. The leader, by contrast, is an environment creator who influences and persuades others, often in an indirect fashion. The leader does not pretend to be the smartest or the toughest or the most knowledgeable. The leader's stock-in-trade is wisdom; the leader listens as much as talks, accepts criticism as well as gives it, exhibits vulnerability rather than looks for it. A leader is passionate, not cynical; enthusiastic, not angry; and inspires confidence, not fear. The executive is the lord of the manor; the leader is its architect.

The end of the organization chart does not mean we have arrived in organizational heaven. While the process-centered organization has some very positive attributes—flexibility, dynamism, and customer focus—it also presents new challenges. Contention and even conflict are endemic to this unavoidably ambiguous new arrangement. As Progressive Insurance's Bruce Marlow says with considerable understatement, it lacks a conventional sort of authority. There's no fixed shape, no single or total responsibility, no straight lines of command—and no simple way to make it work.

In such an environment people will legitimately have different priorities and reach different conclusions that they will need to resolve by give-and-take. Teams are breeding grounds for conflict. Even people who share a common goal will have different views on how to achieve it. The more responsibility that people have for achieving a goal and the more respect that people have for their own views, the more likely and intense such conflict will be. It is when you don't care what happens that you don't expend your energy arguing about it. Nor is such conflict confined to the ranks of process performers. For example, two or more process owners might contend for the same scarce resource. The owners, say, of product development and of order fulfillment might both want an especially qualified finance expert on their team, and both might demand that of the expert's coach. Controversy will also arise between process owners whose processes interface; each has demands to make upon the other.

Since process owners focus on achieving optimal performance today, and since coaches seek to develop human resources for tomorrow, short- and long-term priorities will also unavoidably clash. Consider an engineering coach who feels that the company's direction requires more expertise in high-temperature ceramics. The coach, Bill, informs a process owner, Paul, that after reviewing the company's personnel, he has determined that Jane, an engineer on one of Paul's teams, is best suited to acquire that expertise. Therefore Bill has made arrangements to send Jane to Cal Tech for six months of intensive training. Paul may or may not be interested in high-temperature ceramics; he may not even be terribly interested in Jane. But he *is* extremely concerned about his process, and he may feel that detaching Jane from a team will severely damage its performance. It will take time to find and develop a substitute, and even afterward the loss of Jane may be enduring.

Who's right in this conflict? Process owner Paul, who is

concerned with process performance, or coach Bill, concerned with Jane's development and the longer-term needs of the organization? The answer is that both are right, and if that sounds equivocal, it reflects reality. Once again, this conflict is not the artificially divided loyalties of the matrix. Rather, it reflects the fact that the world is not a simple place, and we often need to try to achieve goals that are not completely consistent.

Clear-cut priorities are rare in the real world. Multiple dimensions and demands are the rule, and there's no secret formula for deciding among them. Actually, conflicts like these have always existed in business organizations, but were hidden by the traditional organizational chart's false simplicity. By unmasking them the process-centered organization compels recognition of the fact that concern with both process and people, customers and costs, and short- and long-term consequences inevitably provokes controversy among well-intentioned people. And it is far better to face than to try to conceal such controversy. Companies have developed a variety of methods for constructively dealing with conflict, from formal negotiation to internal market mechanisms that allow process owners and coaches to bargain and bid for scarce resources. The choice of resolution method matters far less than appreciating that the process-centered world is not a peaceful utopia but a place where healthy conflict is a sign of vitality, passion, and commitment.

CHAPTER 9

Voices from the Front Lines (II)

IN MILITARY maneuvers the troops take to the front lines while the leaders stay back in the bunker and call the shots. But when a company moves to process centering, no one gets to stay back. Everyone is on the front line.

From the executives who assume new leadership roles to the middle managers who must give up supervising and start advising to the performers who take new responsibility for pleasing the customers, everybody faces a new situation. Everyone has a new role, and those new roles require new attitudes and new skills.

In chapter 2 we heard from some process performers about how their working lives have changed. Now we'll hear from a process owner, a coach, and a business leader.

BOB MCMILLAN OF PROGRESSIVE INSURANCE—PROCESS OWNER

In chapter 3 we saw how Progressive Insurance revolutionized its claims process and the work of its adjusters. Bob McMillan, president of Progressive Insurance's Florida division, doubles as the company's claims process leader (owner). Here's how he describes his new role.

Like most success stories, it didn't happen overnight. When we first began the immediate-response claims program back in July 1991, we didn't have any recommended structure mandated for all of our two hundred locations. All we told them was that it's not okay anymore to handle a claim in a week or ten days; from now on, we want you to do it immediately. We got two hundred different approaches to solving that problem. And almost all the locations got in serious workflow difficulties for the first few months.

But we kept watching them all in action until we began to observe that the ones that were working were organized on a team-based approach. So there was nothing elegant about the entire procedure. It was simply a huge exercise in empirical research. Then it fell to the process leaders to look across the country, locate successes, and try to describe them to the rest of our people.

Now we mandate team-based claims resolution throughout the company. We're still at different phases of evolution around the country. In some locations we've made it all the way to a self-managed situation, but in others, teams operate in a way that's pretty traditional, and that seems to work for that location. So there's a fairly wide range, and that's fine with me, as long as it works.

As a process leader I'm in daily contact with the division claim leaders or the senior claims people from our various geographic divisions. My job is to identify the best claims practices in each area, then make recommendations to the nine other divisional presidents, most of whom are also process leaders specializing in other corporate processes. The way it works is that they agree to implement my recommendations on claims issues because that's my background and process specialty. I, in turn, defer to them on whatever their process is.

I also devote a major portion of my day to managing the Florida business. As president of the Florida division I have complete general management responsibility for profit and loss. This dual role is what's unique about our corporate structure.

Bruce Marlow, our COO, is heavily involved in making the final determination about our performance measures in every area. He spends a fair amount of time traveling around to the field organizations, and reports to me, and also to the CEO, on how they're operating in claims. He might say, "I was in the Providence, Rhode Island, area yesterday, and they told me about a method for taking loss reports and dispatching the adjusters." Then he asks whether I think this is a potential process improvement or a waste-causing variance.

In Rhode Island all loss reports were being called in to one central unit with an 800 number rather than to one of several individual claim locations. This seemed like a possibly better way, so we looked more closely and found it was a process improvement, giving some economies from having more people in one location rather than several small groups around the state. So we began to implement that in our other locations. We're constantly looking for ways to streamline and fine-tune the system. It's an open-ended, ongoing process.

Another example is the research we're doing right now on how to match the severity and complexity of a claim event with the right level of expertise for the team member we assign. We're trying to establish processes and indexes by which we can determine the severity of an accident from the first moment a claim is reported. We get around fifty thousand claims a month, so we have to arrive at a simple process for flagging a claim event. Was an emergency medical service or 911 called? Are multiple total-loss vehicles involved? Was it a head-on collision? If any of those elements are present, we'd want to flag the claim. A lot of trauma has occurred here. It's going to be a complex situation, and there's going to be a high level of stress when we get out to the scene, so let's make sure we're dispatching a fully trained, fully experienced representative. But if the loss report says things like "dent," "parking lot involved," or other indicators that it's not a serious event, we don't have to dispatch such an experienced person.

So we're working out a set of trigger words that we can match to each claim representative's experience level. And we're creating some software that will instantly show the experience level and proficiency rating of all our claim representatives. This will also include how many claims they've been assigned in any given twenty-four-hour period and whether they're on field duty that particular day. So I can say, "I have a level-4 claim here. Do I have a level-4 claim representative available?"

Those are the kinds of conceptual things that I work on, all with the larger purpose of compressing time, redesigning for a faster and more accurate claim process. I try to stay out of day-to-day details like telling the division president to use the left-handed or right-handed widget maker.

I happen to like hands-on management, but I satisfy that desire in my role as division president. In our role as process leaders the other division presidents and I have to stay out of the trenches and keep our eyes on the big picture.

I also work closely with the other process leaders in the course of my other job as division president. They're managing me on their processes in the same way that I'm managing and consulting them on mine. For example, the person in charge of the quoting process is also a division president in another part of the country. If my quoting activity in Florida has been deficient, if I'm not getting the quotes done quickly enough or they're not accurate enough, he will call me and ask how he can help with that.

In this instance I'm dealing with him not as another process leader but as a constituent. It could be the other way around tomorrow, when I call him about a claims problem in his division.

In a typical situation I'll be looking at monthly performance data and see response time slipping in a geographic area. So I'll call the claims leader there and ask what's wrong. Is it a staffing or an organizational problem? Is it a resource problem, or are we not organized in the team-based way? We'll brainstorm, and then I'll talk to the division president, or whoever would be my colleague. "John," I'll say, "I've just talked with Paul about this, and I wanted to talk with you, too." And I'll tell John what Paul thinks the problem is: He's a little short on staff and we have to organize another team or appoint a new team leader. I'll tell John, "Paul's working on that, and I'll be monitoring his progress, but I just wanted to let you know that he and I have had this conversation. I'm concerned about it, but I also feel that Paul understands the nature of the problem and has a plan to deal with it."

That's the right way to do it, but I had to arrive there. For a while I went straight to John, but that didn't work because Paul would get upset. And if I went to Paul without informing John afterward, John would get upset. So understanding the correct pathway is very, very important.

I'm outside the divisional structure as a process leader, but I'm also an insider as a division president. So I must be very clear what role I'm playing and make sure it's evenhanded. As claim process leader I'm outside Paul's divisional structure, so I don't decide his salary, but I do have input into what his contingent bonus will be. He doesn't report to me, but I really think you have to earn credibility, and I do that by helping Paul. If he knows I can help him on a problem then I have some credibility with him, which makes me more effective. So the process leader doesn't really get any automatic power. It must be earned.

JIM MARR OF TEXAS INSTRUMENTS—COACH

Texas Instruments is not only becoming a process-centered organization through reengineering, it is using the structures and techniques of process centering in the reengineering effort itself. Jim Marr plays a leadership role in this effort and serves as a coach for a reengineering-related center of excellence.

I have a dual role in our reengineering effort. I'm one of four members of the process and resource leadership team, whose job is to manage the overall reengineering effort. Centers of excellence bring together people with common skills, then enlarge those skills through constant coaching and development. They're the basic building blocks of our reengineering effort. They enable us to assign the right person to the right project at the right time. I'm also a coach for our leadership center of excellence, which is made up of our ninety-five reengineering leaders. I coach about thirty of them.

In our new organization people with common skills and duties—who may, until now, have been in far-flung corners— are grouped together in centers of excellence. The COEs range from advertising to business-programmer analysts to system architects to network engineers. Every skill is represented, and all the leaders in the organization belong to the leadership COE. Everyone has a coach, someone who supports them, as opposed to an old-style boss. Mine is the head of the process and resource leadership team. The coach is the person people go through to set their priorities and get their assignments, but the focus is on long-term growth, helping with skill development. We want to help facilitate the transfer of best practices and knowledge across the organization. In addition coaches assist the project leaders in finding the best available people to staff their projects.

A coach doesn't have to have the same skills as the folks he's coaching. It certainly doesn't hurt, and some knowledge of the skill is essential, but a coach's most important skill is people development: the ability to go in there, really listen, explain what the change is all about, drive home its importance, get people behind it, and get them excited. It's all about having a full-time, hands-on person helping folks develop their potential, as opposed to an old-style manager who had a wider sphere spread across many skills—jack-of-all-trades, master of none.

After a new project is identified and funded by management, it must be staffed. The COE coaches generate lists of qualified people. They know what skills everyone has, and can anticipate any skill gaps that might impede the project. At this point, coaches put together a training plan to bring deficient skills up to what's needed or to teach new skills altogether. In other words, whatever needs to be done to make that project run smoothly, the coach will do. This frees project leaders from bureaucratic hassles so they can concentrate 100 percent on getting the project done well and on time.

We try to avoid pulling people off current projects where their leaving could be disruptive. Our centers of excellence give us a much larger talent pool for looking for the best person. We know they're there, it's a question of finding them and getting them freed up. The coach works with both the new and the old project leader to find an agreeable date that will allow both projects to meet their requirements.

Under the new, project-driven system, units no longer "own" people. In a sense they borrow them from the COE pools. Nobody wants people sitting around who aren't contributing to a project and who have to be funded. The incentive for the project leaders is to make their budget. Previously, managers liked to have lots of people working for them because it looked like they had more responsibility, and would consequently be more highly rewarded.

Middle management was probably the most dramatically threatened by these changes. We used to fund in yearly increments. Once a manager got his staffing and budget approved for the next year, he was free to sit back and run his own show. He knew he was set for a year, so if a cycle time was a little late, Hey, no big deal! Now we select people for a project, they go in and do it, and if they do a good job, we find another assignment for them. We took away the security blanket. The new motivation is: How many projects that really deliver benefit to the corporation can I finish between now and the next performance review? So hanging on to people and dragging out cycle time is no longer helpful in furthering a career.

When we first started to reengineer, some people moved to other parts of the organization to avoid it. Well, it's been so successful that it's spreading everywhere and there's really nowhere to hide. People who can't handle it are leaving the company. As we went through this change, one of the indicators was the ratio of management people to individual contributors. We moved from six or seven to one to twelve to one after the change, and that's counting coaches as management people. This allows us to keep the same number of people, but to have more people doing the meat of the work.

In addition, we reduced our software development cycle time from twenty-two months to thirteen months in the first year, and it's now down to eight months with a target of two months. Everyone is clear about what needs to be done when. Communication is a big part of this: making sure everyone is speaking the same language and has a very clear, concrete understanding of the project goal.

When we reengineered, we set up a theoretical model of how we'd be organized. Then we essentially asked people to give up their old jobs and tell us which jobs they wanted in the new organization. Everyone put down their first, second, and third choices.

We found that although a lot of us believed in the model, nobody really wanted any of the new jobs. Everybody wanted to hang on to their old ones. The problem was, there weren't too many of the old jobs left, so a lot of us were going to have to take the plunge without much hard information about what we were plunging into. Considerable reluctance surfaced. For example, the highest that "coach" got on anyone's wish list was second. I guess it came down to fear of the unknown. As a result we had to do a little gut check to see if we really believed in this thing. After some pretty intense discussion, three of us were convinced to try to be coaches.

In the old organization managers would sit in a room and

do performance evaluations with only their own input. In the new environment the coach delivers the performance message. But there's lots of input; project leaders provide performance feedback, and we also get input from customers, from peers, and from other people who might have some insight into a person's performance. Employees now get what we call 360-degree feedback. The coach's job is to integrate all that and form a constructive discussion process with the individual to help them understand what they're doing well, what they aren't, and what developmental opportunities they have.

One advantage is that project leaders can now be very blunt about someone's performance. They're not telling the person directly but passing it through the coach, who is trained in how to deliver feedback in a constructive manner. We think the quality of feedback has improved. When people have to live with other people there's a tendency to soften any harshness. We dance around weaknesses because of that. Now we get the project leader to give definitive feedback. The coach's job is to find a way to convey the message constructively. Everybody now understands that the worst thing you can do is not tell someone about their developmental opportunities. It doesn't help to sugarcoat the pill because people will think they are capable of doing X and when they are called on to do it they'll fail.

What we really like is when someone comes to us and says, "Look, I know I'm weak in this area. What kind of training is available to help me improve?" Because sometimes people have gaps no one else knows about. If they tell us, we can really help. Look, we all have weaknesses and the best thing to do is face them honestly. Another thing at stake with this feedback is the coach's credibility. If we're not on top of people's real capabilities, if we assign them to a project and they fail, well, the project's in the dump and the coach's credibility is ruined.

In the old organization you didn't share your weaknesses with your manager because they'd be used as a reason to not give you a raise. If you didn't show your weaknesses then theoretically you didn't have any. With coaching, the emphasis is always on improvement and development, in as many areas as possible. We want to turn weakness into strength.

EMMANUEL KAMPOURIS OF AMERICAN STANDARD — BUSINESS LEADER

At American Standard, CEO Emmanuel Kampouris says his job is really continual change management. He sets the goals, defines the targets for the company, and makes sure that what needs to get done gets done. In a highly fluid and intensely competitive world the only way for a company to survive is to keep improving what it does and how it works. The business leader, he says, is the person who prods, cajoles, and makes sure that everyone keeps making the necessary changes. "Your velocity shifts from time to time, but it is always a matter of change and adapting. You become very athletic at it."

When we started to reengineer the manufacturing process in 1990, our aim was to squeeze cycle time out of production. We were moving to "demand-based management," so we needed full flexibility to produce the products when the customers wanted them.

We measure ourselves by inventory turns, which is the ratio you get by dividing the value of your inventories into the value of your annualized cost of goods. When we started, the average of the *Fortune* 500 was about 3.1 or 3.2, and we started with about 3.2 turns. We wanted to double the turns in three years. That essentially meant that we had to halve our inventories. We did this because we were saddled with a lot of debt. We needed millions of dollars in cash to service our debt, which was enormous. We could have survived without cutting inventories, but we would have starved the company of product development and investments in four, five, or six years.

By 1992 we were at about 6.2 turns. We are currently at

about eleven turns and our target is to go to fifteen turns. It means that you have a very well-oiled machine and that your facilities are flexible so they can produce and deliver whatever it is the customer orders.

Even though we have spent four years working with great passion, we are still revising and redesigning. Quite frankly, I don't think it ever ends. In the meantime, in 1992, we decided that if we could improve manufacturing so much, why not do the same thing in the office?

There is always more to do. I think that what happens in reengineering really is that you become very athletic in managing change. You can't let up. From a competitive vantage, you are always in a constant sea of change. Unless an organization is able to assimilate and change rapidly, it will be left behind. What you really want, irrespective of your product, is, ultimately, the right minds.

You can't rest on your laurels for one minute. We are at eleven inventory turns, but we could be up to twenty turns if we did it right. We are on a journey. We have announced that we are a process organization, but the announcement was like firing the first shot to start the race.

It is a constant communications battle. You communicate, then you train and communicate some more. You also need to set very definite objectives of actually producing visible transformations. As a leader I have to reinforce the new things. Because muscles have reflexes, you always tend to go back to your old habits. Especially when things get tough. But you have to stay with it. You have to keep on going forward.

The thing I am talking a lot about these days is co-location. We think that one of the signs that you are really doing reengineering is when you move everybody into one office and have them sitting according to process sequence. We are trying to instill it the way we instilled the importance of inventory turns. It's really the process management that's important; co-location is one of the physical things you can see and touch. The symbolism is as important as the actual work.

For me, the main thing is how I behave. I always ask these

questions in the same order: How are your inventory turns? Where is your co-location? What are you doing? And they know the questions are coming because I am like a broken gramophone. You just keep on asking the questions. I have become more like a preacher than anything else. We still have a long way to go. In all these things, you can talk and pontificate and make speeches. But unless you can reach deep into the hearts of the people and really convince them, you are not going to get anything done.

You have to continue to be passionate about it and keep up the decibels. That's one of the things that really drains you at times. Because you have to wake up in the morning and say, "Here we go again." And sometimes you get bored at hearing yourself speak, pleading, cajoling, and driving people to do these things.

You also focus a lot on incentives. You set the targets, you make some significant incentives, and you communicate. I don't think you can eliminate the incentives. I don't think you can eliminate the passion. I travel a great deal. We have dinners, and we invite people, and we recognize them. We do much more recognition than before. You have to be in a communicating mode and you have to recognize people who do well. More communication—that's probably what has changed the most. And I don't think I am doing a good enough job there quite frankly. You could always do better in communications and encouragement.

We are a global company. We operate in thirty-four countries. Anybody who thinks they can manage a company of our size, with over 54,000 people in thirty-four countries, is wrong. We are very decentralized. The only things we drive centrally are broad programs like reengineering, compensation, and capital expenditures. The rest are decentralized.

What you try to do is to choose the right people to manage and hope that you infiltrate their hearts to drive the systems the way you want. We are all part of the team.

Perhaps the theme that resounds most strongly throughout all these accounts is that process-centered managers play a supportive rather than a controlling role. Whether it is Bob McMillan recommending improved ways of handling claims, Jim Marr helping people recognize areas in need of improvement, or Emmanuel Kampouris encouraging people to maintain the effort for ongoing change, the real center of attention is not management decision making but the work done by the performers. These managers are there to help. Their contribution to the enterprise comes not by supervising or administering but by leveraging the efforts of those on the front lines.

It is also clear that the transition to a process-centered environment is not an easy one, neither for performers nor for managers. Old styles and behaviors have to be discarded, and unfamiliar ones must be adopted. This change is not a superficial one because behind these new behaviors there must be new attitudes and beliefs, new value systems to motivate and encourage the new behaviors. In other words, it is in the hearts and souls of the people in an organization that process centering must take hold if it is to succeed. It is therefore to the collective spirit of the process-centered enterprise that we now turn our attention.

PART III

ENTERPRISE

CHAPTER 10

THE SOUL OF A NEW COMPANY

A CORPORATION is more than a collection of processes, more than a set of products and services, even more than an association of people at work. It is also a human society, and like all societies, it nourishes particular forms of culture—"corporate cultures." We're all familiar with this notion. Every company has its own language, its own version of its history (its myths), and its own heroes and villains (its legends), both historical and contemporary. The whole flourishing tangle serves to confirm old-timers and to induct newcomers in the corporation's distinctive identity and its particular norms of behavior. In myriad ways, formal and informal, it tells them what is okay—and what is not.

Despite their many differences, there are great similarities across most contemporary corporate cultures. Certain themes resonate almost everywhere: avoiding blame and responsibility, treating co-workers as competitors, feeling entitled, and not feeling intense and committed. This commonality is hardly surprising. After all, most of today's corporations were born and raised in the same business environment, subject to the same pressures and issues. And because nurture definitely dominates nature in the business world, most companies, facing a common context, developed a common culture.

The key feature of the environment in which most contemporary organizations came of age is that, by and large, for the last two hundred years demand exceeded supply. It would be an exaggeration to say that corporate growth in this era was purely demographic—a simple matter of the growing numbers and purchasing power of consumers—but it wouldn't be much of one. On the whole, from the last quarter of the eighteenth century to the last quarter of the twentieth century, producers have consistently had the upper hand over consumers. Except during downturns in the business cycle, there were always more people—or companies—who wanted to buy than there were goods or services to satisfy them. Whether it was automobiles, telephone service, or soft drinks, the dominant concern for the modern corporation has been to keep up with apparently insatiable demand.

This demand shaped the world's business environment and shaped virtually everything about corporate cultures. The corporate way to success was not to innovate—that was the job of the entrepreneur—but to harness an earlier innovation and to ramp it up in scale in order to meet demand that could safely be assumed to be waiting. The primary goal was not making mistakes. With a market waiting to be taken, brilliance and innovation were unnecessary; caution and plodding could be counted on to carry the day. So why take risks? The highest values were those of planning, control, and discipline—the values needed to capitalize on a ready market.

This business context fostered company cultures that were strangely at odds with America's independent and democratic spirit. You might suppose that nothing could go more against the American grain than having to make a career, or at least a living, in organizations that were at once paternalistic, controlling, and bureaucratic. Here was a hat trick, if there ever was one, against personal freedom! Yet so it was for everyone except those lucky few who scrambled their way through bureaucratic warrens and up the hierarchical pole. Most everyone else, workers and managers alike, found life in the industrial era corporation stifling and disheartening. Inventiveness was frustrated by protocol and work rules. Ambition expressed itself more in politics than in productivity. Craftsmanship was a thing of the past, and creativity a thing of the future—for afterhours.

If you believe (as many people do) that work, what you do in life as a producer of goods and services for your fellow man, is the decisive constituent of your identity and selfworth, then work in the culture of an industrial era corporation could be—could still be—very bad for you. For two hundred years the primary demand on the employee was to work hard, obey the boss or shop steward, follow the rules, and keep your nose clean (and down). This may have been "rational," at least from the point of view of the company. A demographically growing market sponsors a task-centered organization, which in turn fosters work that's routine and simple. If each individual works hard and obediently at his or her task, the organization will succeed. Diligence is all that's called for. But "rational" though it may have been, this culture had devastating effects on the spirits and psyches of many who had to work in it.

If work in an industrial era company culture was bad for you, why did people put up with it for so many years? The answer is obvious—security. Even Americans were never so in love with freedom, independence, and risk—were never, in a word, so *entrepreneurial*—that they would blithely brush aside the value of employment security. To oversimplify (but again not by much): At the heart of the old company culture was a deal—obedience and diligence in exchange for security. The deal was not always arrived at simply: Many workers had to unionize and strike to get real security (not to mention higher pay); management had to supervise and bureaucratize to get the other side of the bargain. But the deal was there, and it held for the better part of the modern era.

No longer. An historic chain reaction is under way—enormous change in the business environment forcing deep changes in company cultures—and the cumulative effect is a deal-breaker. The rise of the demanding customer is the crucial precipitating factor in the chain reaction that is doing in the security for obedience and diligence deal. Corporate managers once had but one master in the business environment— their investors. Now they have two, investors and customers. Debating their relative power over the fate of an enterprise is like asking which is more important, food or shelter. You must have both. But from a decision-making point of view there's no question about which of these masters comes first. It is the customer: Acquire and satisfy customers and you'll attract and satisfy investors.

When the customer comes first in the environment, something has to adjust in the company culture. The customer cares nothing for our management structure, our strategic plan, our financial structure—or for the culture that revered these artifacts. The customer is interested in one thing only: results, the value we deliver to him or her. This is of course the genesis of the process-centered organization. A customer focus forces an emphasis on results, hence on the processes that produce results, hence on developing an organizational structure that centers on processes—and on fashioning a culture that supports them.

The effect of the modern customer on the security for obedience and diligence deal has been slow in coming, but it can be felt already. Hands are what employees used to be called, and as hands they were treated. Their every motion, down to the tiniest twitch of muscle, was commanded by the managerial brain. To be sure, the hands were also well cared for, protected by union and other contracts. They were also protected by a carefully cultivated ignorance of the marketplace, and more or less shielded from its vicissitudes. These hands knew their place and they kept it. They willingly exchanged their hearts—and perhaps their souls—for a contract and guaranteed wage increase.

But now with the ascendancy of the customer, both aspects of this treatment—the commands and the protection—have become disastrous. When a customer calls the tune, everyone in a company must dance. But this means letting go of commands. No system that depends on segregating wisdom and decision-making into a managerial class can possibly offer the speed and agility customers demand. It also means letting go of metaphors like "hands." Processes require whole human beings possessed of hands, heads, and hearts to perform them.

If commands have to go, so do protections. In the new regime managers do not decide the fate of employees—customers do. The company does not close plants or lay off workers—customers do, by their actions or inactions. Samuel Gompers might plausibly throw his slogan of "More!" in the face of a monopolist or oligopolist. His antagonists controlled their markets and their customers; if they wished, they could give employees a bigger cut of their pie. Now it verges on the comical to read screeds against "giant and powerful multinational corporations." The corporations I know are closer to "pitiful helpless giants," all running scared of their customers. Supermarkets dictate delivery terms to mighty consumer-goods manufacturers; pharmaceutical companies must yield to the cost-containment demands of managed care providers; large borrowers go around the banks rather than to them; long-distance carriers watch helplessly as subscribers switch allegiances overnight. Companies are afraid that customers will desert for an established competitor, that they will transfer their allegiances to an aggressive start-up, that they will demand more for less. When the customer comes first, the company and its employees must perforce come second. Our needs must be subordinated to those of the people for whom we are creating value.

Like it or not, security, stability, and continuity are out because there simply isn't anyone on the scene who can provide them. The company can't because the customer won't. Companies are not cold or cruel or heartless. They are merely running as fast as they can to keep up with demanding and unforgiving customers. The people who work in them will have to do the same. It's not that no one cares about you; it's just that there is nothing anyone can do about it.

But the new regime also offers compensation for the withdrawal of the power of command (from managers) and the withdrawal of protection from customers and the market (from all employees). It offers freedom and personal growth. The essence of the new deal in the process-centered organization is an exchange—initiative for opportunity. The company offers its employees the opportunity—and often the educational means—to achieve personal success. In return, the employee promises the company to exercise initiative in creating value for customers and thereby profits for the company.

Obedience and diligence are now irrelevant. Following orders is no guarantee of success. Working hard at the wrong thing is no virtue. When customers are kings, mere hard work—work without understanding, flexibility, and enthusiasm—leads nowhere. Work must be smart, appropriately targeted, and adapted to the particular circumstances of the process and the customer. Imagination, flexibility, and commitment to results are what's needed. If the results aren't achieved, you can no longer claim, "But I did what I was told and I worked very hard." It doesn't matter. You are accountable for results, not for effort.

Without protection there is no reason to obey, and with obedience goes its cousin, loyalty. "Loyalty to company" as a cultural artifact is replaced by "commitment to business success." The quasi-feudal assumption of the "organization man"—that putting the interests of the company first was dispensation from further responsibility and guaranteed personal success—is now ridiculous. Without results, without business success, loyalty is an empty gesture. Since it no longer guarantees success for the organization, it can no longer guarantee success for the individual. Loyalty and hard work are by themselves quaint relics, about as important to contemporary business success as the ability to make a perfect dry martini. Indeed, organizations must now urge employees to put loyalty to the customer over loyalty to the company—because that is the only way the company will thrive.

In a task-centered organization "satisfactory performance" was all that could be expected from employees, and it was all that was truly needed. Fragmented processes so homogenized individual work that outstanding personal performance would inevitably be bleached out in the wash. The final result was only as good as the worst link in the chain that produced it. In such a context, making a strong effort was likely to be a waste. So why bother? It was far more important to avoid mistakes than to excel. This is not the case in process-centered organizations. High-performing process performers can produce a high-performance result. Adequacy no longer suffices. Excellence is required.

These shifts in norms are under way in a great many companies. They represent a radical transformation of the culture of modern organizations, the nexus of values that drives behavior. A few, such as GTE, have even made them explicit. At GTE a passive worker's role has given way to an active one. "Compliance and support"—following orders—has been replaced by "decisiveness." Each individual worker now has the responsibility to do whatever it takes to assure successful process outcome. Instead of "flexibility to move or retrain," in which the employee agrees to accept what the company mandates for him, GTE now expects "flexibility to learn and relearn." It is now the employee's responsibility to take an active role in his or her own future, career, and skills development. I am the object of your training, but the actor in my own learning. Instead of promising "a lifetime of work," the employee must now commit to a "readiness to change."

Similar changes are also under way in GTE's commitments to its employees. No longer is the company the "head," the employee the "hand." The employee is now assumed to be a mature, capable, self-reliant adult. The company does not promise to take care of the employee—which is just as well, since such a promise would be a false and empty one. "Taking care of one's employees" implies a degree of control over one's environment—that one can really shelter people from external forces and their impacts. This promise may have been realistic once but is laughable now. Instead of protection the company owes its people opportunity: the chance to do well, to succeed, to grow in one's career.

At GTE this means that "paternalistic management" gives way to "candid leadership." These words are well chosen. The company no longer "manages" its people; the term reeks of passivity, of victimization, of abdication of personal responsibility. Leadership, by contrast, provides people with the vision, motivation, and context they need in order to succeed. But it demands action and responsibility on everyone's part.

Real leadership must be candid. Truth-telling was not an important value in the traditional organization. "Hands" had to be told only what they should do; telling them more might confuse or paralyze them, and was certainly a waste of time. But it is immoral to deceive human beings (and difficult to deceive educated ones). If people are to make the best decisions for themselves, they must be given as much information as possible. It is not enough for me to stop pulling your strings, I must be sure that you can pull them yourself.

Thus, "on the job training" now gives way to "information about the business." GTE may or may not be able to offer employees continued employment, but it does owe them full information about what the business needs so they can make their own assessments of their prospects and plan accordingly.

No longer can "promotion from within" be taken for granted. In a world of change and unpredictability, who can say what talents the company will need and where they will be found? The company can no longer promise that new opportunities will go first to existing employees, for they may not have the capabilities needed to discharge them. Instead, GTE now promises "opportunity for development," with opportunity again being the critical word. We'll promise you a chance, but that's all we can promise.

Instead of "training and retraining"—once again a model in which the employee is the object of external forces—the new deal is "a training climate and the offer of training." Should a GTE employee leave the company, he or she should be able to do so a more capable and knowledgeable individual than on arrival.

But there's a proviso to this: *provided* he or she takes advantage of the opportunity. Process professionals must coldly appraise every employment situation for the opportunities it offers for personal development as well as for its immediate compensation. "Candidly, you have people understand that there is less likelihood they'll remain with one company over their career," says Bruce Carswell, GTE's recently retired senior vice president of human resources. Whether they're at GTE for five years or thirty depends on their continuing *self*-development. Gone is the notion that "somehow the company has the obligation to develop you." In any case, Carswell urged GTE employees to "look for the opportunities to broaden your professional portfolio while you're with us.

That will be an asset for you whether you stay here or go somewhere else."

Not everything at GTE is changing. Employees are still expected to exhibit "ethical and honest behavior," and the company must continue to offer "fair and respectful treatment" and a "safe and healthy workplace." But the differences far outweigh the continuities. GTE is operating in a new way, and it feels like a very different place. The company's culture—its very soul—has been transformed.

Whether these changes are good or bad is a value judgment that must be made by every individual. Some will consider the new regime to be liberating and empowering. They will see it as conveying dignity and autonomy to every employee by eliminating the controlling and confusing network of rules that have confined most people in their work lives. Others will see it as a harsh and cruel new world, a Darwinian jungle where only the fittest survive—and that only temporarily.

I prefer to simply call it realistic. For too long the large organization provided a fantasy environment in which people pretended that there was such a thing as security. By working hard and following the rules the uncertainties of the outside world could be kept at bay. The organization provided a buffer against reality, a comfortable zone of predictability and stability. So long as demand exceeded supply and customers were docile and subservient, the fantasy could continue. No more. Large corporations now do not dominate their landscapes—controlling their customers and securely deciding their own futures—any more than start-ups do. The large company and its employees must get used to the environment and lifestyle to which their entrepreneurial cousins adapted long ago—an environment of uncertainty and anxiety, but also of exhilarating freedom. It may not be to everyone's liking, but there is no going back.

In effect, the qualitative difference between large companies and small ones, between young companies and established ones, between those who create markets and those who control them, is gone. It has been replaced by a mere quantitative difference. Large businesses are no longer very different from small ones; to paraphrase Hemingway's comment to Fitzgerald, they simply have more people. And if a large corporation is, in effect, becoming more like a small company, then everyone who works in it must start acting and thinking like an owner of a small company. Our new role model is no longer the corporate manager but the entrepreneur. No one needs to tell the small company owner of the need to stay close to the customer, to remain flexible, to reduce non-value-adding overhead, to respond quickly to new situations. He or she sees with absolute clarity the connection between business performance and personal success and future prospects. The small businessperson will do whatever it takes to succeed, knowing that the past is no indicator of the future, that the luxury of coasting does not exist, that there is no guarantee of future employment, and that success at one thing means nothing without success at everything else.

This holistic perspective, this visceral connection with the marketplace and the consequences of one's own actions, is now required of every single employee. A refrain that I hear daily is that everyone must think and behave like an owner. This is not achieved merely through equity participation, ownership of some shares in the company. Though that is helpful, the feedback it provides is often too deferred to matter. It is through tying everyone's compensation to the performance of their process and to the company as a whole—as was described in chapter 4—that people's attitudes are recentered.

Even this is not enough. One of the most important emerging themes in business today is broad-based business education and understanding. If everyone is to think and act like an owner, then everyone must have an owner's perspective on the business. They must understand the company as a whole, not just one small part of it. They must appreciate the factors driving the industry. They must know the issues shaping the competitive marketplace. Companies are finding that this requires a major commitment to business education for the workforce. Truck drivers must understand the economics of the distribution process so they can explain to small customers why they pay more for products than big customers. Customer service representatives must know how customers use their products so they can act as an aftermarket sales force. Factory workers must understand the origins and destinations of the products they are making.

Such knowledge is not of theoretical value. Understanding shapes attitudes and attitudes shape behavior—and change in behavior is ultimately what process centering is all about. Broad-based business education is an unprecedented undertaking for most companies, and it will not come for free. A typical number I hear is that companies are increasing their education budgets by a factor of four or five for this new era.

The need for such education is obvious to anyone willing to ask some simple questions. When I visit companies, I like to ask rank and file and middle managers alike the following: Who are this company's five most important customers? How is your industry changing? What are the crucial issues the company must address if it is to succeed in the next five years? By and large, I get blank stares in response. Such issues aren't seen as the concern of the purchasing department, the shipping group, or customer service. Such "business" questions have until now been left only to the most senior executives. Now they must be everyone's concern. Businesses need businesspeople, not functionaries, and they must educate their people to that end.

The culture of a process-centered organization must also encourage people to accept the inevitability of tension and even conflict. I'm not referring to the old political infighting and back-stabbing, the turf protection and empire building, of corporate Byzantiums. Rather, I refer to the conflict that inevitably arises when independent people must work together to achieve multiple objectives in an environment of flux, ambiguity, and scarce resources.

As we said in chapter 8, it is possible to fashion various mechanisms for coping with conflict. But better yet would be for the organization to fashion a culture that appreciates the creative power of conflict and seeks to harness it. Common objectives, mutual respect, and a true team spirit help shape a context in which conflict is recognized as a sign of vital life, not an aberration or a symptom of organizational breakdown.

A tolerance for risk is another aspect of the process-centered organization that runs counter to traditional corporate cultures. Ann Dronen of Commerce Clearing House articulates the new requisite attitude when she stresses the need to constantly encourage people to take more risks and "put their butts on the line." Dronen acknowledges that the residue of the old school's fear of making mistakes—reflective of a deeper assumption that that was the only way to get fired—is hard to eliminate entirely. The key to success in eradicating risk-averse behavior is for management to send out a clear signal that "we aren't going to condemn people for taking gambles, as long as their intentions were good and the effort was there." Bruce Marlow of Progressive Insurance concurs. "We never punish people for failure. We only punish sloppy execution and the failure to recognize reality."

Bob Lehmann, a senior project manager for AT&T, remembers a second-level plant manager "breathing down your throat in the old days, and every time there was a mistake, he'd yell and scream." Unsurprisingly, in such environments people would go to great lengths to avoid admitting the existence of problems or taking responsibility for them. Now, by contrast, surfacing a problem does not diminish respect for the person grappling with it, "and there hasn't been any retribution."

Deborah Smithart, Brinker International's executive vice president and CFO, makes the same point about the correlation between higher confidence, increased responsibility, and a more mature attitude toward miscalculations. "In the past managers had enough layers above them that they just kept kicking it up until somebody else approved it. Now, you really don't have that luxury. But making decisions means you have an environment where some mistakes occur. Making a mistake used to mean you were fired or ostracized. Today it's more like if you don't see a person making mistakes, they're probably not pushing hard enough to look for new opportunities." Process-centered companies must remember the counterintuitive dictum that winners make more mistakes than losers—because winners, striving for great gains, occasionally take missteps, while losers never do because they never try.

How do all these new cultural elements look when they're brought together? For that, let's look at GPU Generation Corporation (Genco), a medium-sized electric power producer that operates plants in New Jersey and Pennsylvania. Their previously regulated and monopolistic industry is now in the throes of deregulation, and the company is converting to a process-centered structure to enable it to keep up. A cross section of people from across the company have worked together to articulate the kinds of attitudes and philosophies that everyone will need to share if the company is to make it. The following are some excerpts from their work:

"In the GPU Generation Corporation our only measure of success is to find out who our primary paying customers are (or will be), find out what they want, and give it to them at a better overall value than anyone else."

"*Nothing we do is more important than creating the best value for our customers. No other work matters at all.*"

"*Serving and creating value for the customer means that each member of the firm must be treated as a professional who, whenever possible, is in charge of the whole job, not just pieces of it. Stop checking with the boss. You know what's best and you have an obligation to serve your customer and not keep asking for permission. If you need assistance, ask for it.*"

"*To be effective, you must have both freedom and autonomy while at the same time acting professionally.*"

"*If we are successful at becoming truly focused on creating value for our customers, we shouldn't need bosses in the traditional sense at all. We will already know what to do. We will need only to be kept informed and coached so we can be even more effective at what we do.*"

"*Nobody hands us anything. We work for what we have, every day. We can't stand for anyone who does not want to contribute to our team.*"

This is not theory, this is reality. The process-centered organization is characterized by responsibility, autonomy, risk, and uncertainty. It may not be a gentle environment, but it is a very human one. Gone are the artificial rigidities and disciplines of the conventional corporation. In its place is a world full of the messiness, challenges, and disappointments that characterize the real world of real human beings.

CHAPTER 11

CORPORATE JERICHO

THE DEMOLITION of the Berlin Wall is a potent symbol of our times and not just of the end of the Cold War. Rigid barriers of all sorts—from armed frontiers to corporate boundaries to the neat distinctions our minds have made for the last few hundred years—are crumbling overnight. Our old structures were designed like strongholds, to withstand attack. They were armor-plated, like some dim-witted, lumbering Jurassic reptile. Modern structures—in business, in society, in politics—must be open and flexible if they are to keep up with the pace of change. To use a military analogy, old corporate structures resembled those of cold war armies—massive, centralized, and focused on a well-defined enemy. New structures must be more like rapid deployment forces, able to go wherever needed and to get there fast.

Process centering is about tearing down walls. The boundaries of organizations are becoming more flexible, permeable, and dynamic; it is increasingly hard to find them at all. Focusing on process means rejecting compartmentalization and dissolving functional boundaries. On a process team there are no walls. Indeed we deliberately avoid the familiar term "cross-functional team" because it places too much emphasis on the functions, making it seem as though the team is a collection of mutually suspicious partisans representing different functions. The centers of excellence, the old functions with the work removed and people's concerns brought to the fore, are really cross-process support groups for process teams. The old, clear-cut borders between functions have become attenuated.

Visit a company and observe a group of people working on, say, product development. If you can't tell who belongs to what center of excellence, you've stumbled into a process-centered environment. On a process team, engineering, marketing, manufacturing, and finance people have a common goal and their lines of responsibility are not restrictively defined. (Note we do *not* say "people *from* finance, engineering, etc." Finance is someone's profession, not his or her allegiance.) A finance expert may have helpful suggestions about product design. An engineer may have insight into market needs, and so on.

Even boundaries between teams make little sense. When, for example, the output of a manufacturing process is among the inputs of the order fulfillment process, the two must see each other as allies, not adversaries. A barrier between the two would represent precisely the kind of obstruction that process centering seeks to remove in the first place. Replacing functional silos with process tunnels would be little improvement.

However, a focus on process dissolves more than in-house boundaries. *All* business boundaries are crumbling. The corporate world has long been a bastion of a kind of tribalism, rooted in an "us against them" mentality in which the "us" shifted with circumstances from the organization as a whole to one's narrowly defined part of it—while "them" was everywhere. Fighting the competition was never enough. Many companies acted as though customers and suppliers were worse enemies than their competitors. Bob Lutz, president of Chrysler, uses feudal imagery when he says that Chrysler used to treat its suppliers as serfs. After all, it was often easier to increase revenue by pressuring suppliers for price concessions or sticking a short-handed customer with a price increase than to outperform the competition on the field of battle. And many business units reserved their most intense acrimony for their supposedly "fellow" business units within the same corporation. Internal competition for resources, approvals, and promotions was often far more intense than any external competition. After all, in an era of growing markets, there's enough business for everyone, but there are only so many seats at the top table. All this was based on an understanding of business as a zero-sum game in which you succeed only when others fail—which is about as appropriate today as wearing spats to an MTV job interview.

Let's first consider the breaching of intercompany boundaries, then return to the internal ones.

Corporate walls have traditionally been high, hard, and heavily guarded. We can think of corporations as fortified castles that transacted arms-length business with each other. Typically, companies defined themselves in terms of a discrete set of products and services—making valves, distributing snack foods, or insuring middle-income clients. Their inputs included orders from customers, raw materials from suppliers, and various forms of market intelligence. Within the castle these inputs were processed to produce outputs that were tossed over the walls as products and services for customers and payments to suppliers. The company's processes were self-contained; they began and ended at the company ramparts. The classical strategy of integration was one of expanding the castle walls so as to encompass even more within it.

The worldview implicit in this model is that of *Leviathan* (1651), in which the English philosopher Thomas Hobbes described human society as a "war of everyone against everyone," where everyone is everyone else's enemy. When customers and suppliers as well as competitors are one's enemies, and the goal is to maximize one's own performance and profit, the only way to achieve success is at the expense of the neighboring castles. Build the walls higher and stronger, do more for yourself, depend not on others, and take advantage of every sign of weakness to extend the domain of the realm: These were the mottoes of the feudal corporation.

This is not a prelude to a call for a kinder, gentler way of doing business, but rather for a more intelligent way. The disadvantage of defensive and hostile relationships with all external parties is that they breed the same kind of problems "out there" that we have sought to eliminate "in here." High walls between corporations, with their attendant secrecy and tight control, cause much waste of time and effort. When my customer and I both treat our inventory levels as state secrets, both our inventory levels escalate. When my purchasing system produces a requisition that must be converted into an order and reentered into my supplier's order processing system, redundant work is widespread, delay is inevitable, and errors are rampant. When my component supplier is given the specifications for his component but not one drop more of information about my product into which his component must fit, opportunities for synergy, integration, and reuse are lost.

Mutual suspicion leads us to line our corporate ramparts with guards to warn of any approach. Lack of trust compels us to spend as much effort checking, weighing, and inspecting as in doing our real—i.e., value-adding and creative—work. The overheads of wary relationships are enormous. The same work, such as quality checking, is performed on both sides of an intercompany interface, when goods are shipped and again when they are received. The quality of information also suffers. Information is guarded, and only aggregate data is passed up the chain of customers and suppliers, causing patterns to blur and details to be lost, and leaving only a crude appreciation of what's really happening at the end of the line.

Moreover, assets and inventories proliferate. When we are unsure of our customers' ordering patterns, we build up finished goods inventory, just in case someone decides to order from us. When customers are unsure of our ability to fill their orders, they build up their inventory in case we fail. The result is the accumulation of goods in multiple warehouses and vast duplication of effort, including but not limited to rehandling of goods.

This need not be so. A process perspective can apply to processes that involve two (or more) companies as well as to those that operate within a single company. If we ignore corporate boundaries and rethink a system from the end result back—that is, starting with satisfying the ultimate customer—we often see that the total process that produces that end result involves a number of companies, each performing a part of the process. Drawing lines divides this unitary process into multiple ones. Arbitrarily following corporate boundaries creates unnecessary fragmentation, with all the problems we've mentioned and more. It's as if a single airplane flight were operated by three airlines: one for takeoff, one for cruising, and one for landing.

To take a more down-to-earth example, a person who enters a supermarket to buy a bag of potato chips is really a customer of what has become known as an integrated supply chain process. This process begins with the chip maker, who orders potatoes, oil, and salt. (Or we might even say it begins with the producers of these commodities.) The chip maker manufactures and bags the product. Then the trucking company takes over, picking up the boxes, determining the best shipping routes, and delivering the chips to the supermarket chain's distribution center where they are stored and scheduled for delivery to individual supermarkets. Customers are supremely uninterested in the number of companies involved in this process. They need a process that puts chips in their hands for the final short trip to the mouth. But it does matter that three distinct, mutually suspicious entities have raised the cost and decreased the freshness of the chips by spending enormous amounts of time and money duplicating each other's efforts and wasting energy in overcoming the inevitable friction at their boundaries.

Companies and industries are recognizing that they must not focus on the artificial subprocesses that begin and end at company boundaries, but rather on whole processes that cross corporate walls. This phenomenon has been called "customer-supplier partnership" or "the virtual corporation," but such terms are inadequate. Partnership usually implies trust, goodwill, and good feelings, but we do not expect a sudden infusion of the commercial world with selflessness and brotherhood. On the contrary, we suggest that a focus on intercorporate processes can only be motivated by enlightened self-interest. Nor would the sudden spreading of sweetness and light get the potato chips to the shelf any faster. The goal is not to change the way companies *feel* about their trading partners but the ways they *interact* with them. Better interaction may well serve to modify feelings later as a consequence of mutual benefit received. But the tangible things, the underlying hard systems of operations, must be changed first.

The place to begin is to recognize what constitutes the larger, intercorporate process. For example, at GE's Large Appliance division the line separating the company from its retailers used to be quite clear. GE made home appliances—let's think of refrigerators here—and sold them to retailers. The retailers in turn sold them to consumers. GE's goal was to sell its retailers as many refrigerators as possible at the best price while incurring the least cost in doing so. But the unexpected rise of mass merchandisers subverted that approach. Vast chains like Wal-Mart exert great power over their suppliers and have the clout to demand low prices and favorable terms. On the other hand, GE's smaller retail customers found it difficult to compete against the chains' low overheads and razor-thin margins.

GE recognized that if it didn't do something to sustain its smaller retailers, the outlets for its products would be disastrously reduced. Dumping inventory on retailers and letting *them* worry about what to do with it would no longer work. GE responded by taking a broad view of the process that begins with manufacturing and ends with a purchase by the consumer. In essence, GE has assumed overall inventory management responsibility for this process, thereby virtually eliminating the need for its retailers to keep their own inventory of major appliances, apart from a handful of demonstration models. This has been accomplished by means of a computerized system called "Direct Connect." When a customer wants to buy a refrigerator, retailers use Direct Connect to check availability and price. The order is entered into Direct Connect, and next-day delivery to the consumer is filled not from dealer inventory but from GE's own supply of finished goods.

This redefinition of its relationship with its retailers also provides a mechanism for GE to offer financing directly to the purchaser without the dealer serving as an intermediary. In return for the advantages (lower inventory and less work) that this new process offers them, GE retailers commit to carrying a full line of GE product categories and to ensure that GE items will represent at least 50 percent of their appliance sales. The retailers who use Direct Connect also pay GE monthly by electronic transfer, reducing GE's billing and invoicing costs and providing more rapid access to cash.

This is a classic win/win arrangement. The retailers benefit because they are able to respond quickly to customer orders while being freed from inventory management and delivery responsibility for many products. They don't have to process credit applications either. GE has solidified its market share while achieving a significant cost reduction in its own distribution and marketing activities. By adding more value to the retailer, GE has generated great loyalty and improved its own operational efficiency. This is a direct result of looking at the whole of a process, instead of breaking it into two loosely connected parts, and committing to the goal of performing it at lowest total cost with the highest customer satisfaction. Breaching the intercorporate boundary allowed the freest and most intelligent placement of work—GE doing work that had been performed by the retailer and vice versa.

Traditional organizations have operated under a very simple rule of thumb: whoever benefited from work should perform it. If it is my inventory, then it is my problem to manage it; if the design is yours, then you should worry about how to manufacture it. This attitude was perfectly attuned to the Hobbesian beggar-thy-neighbor style that used to prevail. The idea of doing more than the absolute minimum, of performing work that benefited another, smacked of altruism and charity, not business. We are now starting to recognize this as the narrow and ultimately futile approach that it is. Work should be done by whoever is best equipped to do it—whichever organization has the best skills, the most convenient opportunity, the right data or software, or even the most intense interest. Rather than just focusing on the narrow work that must be conducted within its walls, a company should seek to improve, however it can, the overall performance of the larger, boundary-crossing process. Why? Because driving out cost, increasing value, and speeding cycle times of this larger process will ultimately rebound to the benefit of all organizations involved in it. Virtue may or may not be its own reward, but doing good for my trading partners will do well for me, too. The opportunities for optimization of a total, multicompany process exceed those that can be achieved merely by optimizing each of its single-company constituent processes.

This trend is not the future—it is already the present. The transportation industry in particular is already evolving from mere truck drivers to materials managers who operate in tight synchronization with their customers, the manufacturers whose goods are being moved. Many truck-leasing companies were originally founded as financial devices—to take advantage of tax law provisions—for firms that needed truck fleets but hesitated to invest the required capital to acquire them. These companies began by simply buying and leasing trucks; they are now increasingly integrating themselves into their customers' operations and assuming more and more responsibility for them. The first step was full-service leasing: taking responsibility for maintenance, fuel, insurance, licensing, etc., of the leased trucks. The next step was dedicated-contract carriage wherein drivers, labor management, and distribution system design were also provided. Ryder Truck, for instance, has recognized that its customers don't want trucks, they want goods to be moved as effectively as possible from one site to another. To this end Ryder provides its customers with least-cost routing software to determine the best route by which goods can be moved, vehicle planning systems to advise on where the vehicles should be based according to expected traffic patterns, and maintenance management systems to help customers get the most road time out of trucks at the lowest maintenance cost.

For most manufacturers—whose focus should be on the key processes of understanding customers, developing technologies, and designing and making products—transportation logistics are a distraction. Although they must get their product to market at the end of the day, it scarcely pays to develop leading-edge know-how and practices in the arcana of truck maintenance and traffic management. Using other companies whose expertise is precisely those specialties is far more sensible.

This goes beyond outsourcing, or simply lopping off staff activities and assigning them to a third-party vendor. Various companies can bring various strengths to bear at various points in an end-to-end-process. The total process is therefore best performed by a kind of corporate consortium, each member contributing its special expertise. As technology advances and competitive pressures grow, it is less realistic than ever for companies to think they can be world-class at everything—and being second-rate at anything threatens competitive performance. It's no good saying, "Never mind about *that* because we excel at *this*." Of course electronics companies must have state-of-the-art technology, but without state-of-the-art distribution that offers superior delivery at the lowest costs customers will soon be as dissatisfied as if product features were obsolete—especially as some eager competitor will be happy to assure them they don't have to choose between features and delivery. Since *everything* must be done excellently, the question becomes what to do for yourself and what you should have others do for you.

This principle can also be seen at work in the health insurance industry, which began as largely an indemnity business. Corporations turned to insurers to assume the risk associated with their employees' health. After the premium was paid it was the insurer's problem. But over time it became clear that merely taking on risk was not always a significant added value.

Spreading risk by combining many small populations into a large population was the classical *raison d'être* of the insurance company. Reducing a small population's statistical uncertainty provided a degree of security for everyone, but many large corporations came to realize that they didn't need this service. Their employees represented statistical universes on their own. Spreading that risk any further didn't do much good—and if your own population was for the most part young, healthy, and vigorous, it might even be disadvantageous. So corporations began assuming their own risk, with many group health insurers turning into ASO (Administrative Services Only) providers. Those insurers essentially became claims processors for their clients, managing but not owning the bank accounts that paid for medical costs. In other words, the tide flowed back to the corporate customers who assumed some work (such as risk management) previously performed by their insurance providers.

Now the tide has begun to reverse its flow. Many health insurance companies have become managed care companies, often still not indemnifying their clients for medical costs—self-insurance remains the rule—but operating as consultants to ensure that the clients minimize their health-care expenditures, which is no insignificant issue for many companies. (Many manufacturers spend more on health care than on raw materials.) By evaluating alternative providers, offering second opinions, and recommending wellness and other programs to avoid a need for medical care in the first place, the insurers have begun to break the back of health-care cost inflation. Thus the overall process of providing health-care benefits to employees has been redivided between employers and insurers, with the employer taking the risk the insurer used to assume and the insurer taking over work that the employer would otherwise be forced to do. This new relationship is reinforced by several advantages insurers have over their clients. For one thing, any individual client's data covers only its own medical expenses and costs, whereas insurers know far more from the large number of people and companies they serve. Secondly, even management of their employees' health-care costs is fundamentally a distraction for virtually all companies. The energy devoted to containing those costs is better spent elsewhere.

Similar arrangements abound in other industries. Saturn's suppliers have essentially taken over the company's materials management, allowing it to concentrate on efficient car manufacturing. Saturn posts its production schedules in an on-line database. The suppliers are responsible for seeing that the right goods are delivered to the right bay of the plant at the right time to ensure unbroken production. In return Saturn has tipped its hand, allowing its suppliers to see its production schedule and assuring them of a market.

Levi Strauss & Co. uses its LeviLink services to advise a number of its retailers on what products and sizes they ought to be carrying. It does this by analyzing their sales of Levi's jeans, Dockers, and other products in comparison to prior sales at their outlets. Levi Strauss can then suggest exactly what models, colors, and sizes the retailers should reorder and when. In many cases the company goes further by taking the initiative and creating the order, thereby relieving the retailer of all responsibility and involvement in the order creation process. The goods even arrive preticketed, ready to go directly onto the retailers' shelves.

Again, this is doing what you do best. You may be best at something because of particular skills, because you do it in greater volume than anyone else, because you have an advantage based on special technology in which you have invested, or because it is important enough for you to put in the time and energy to do it better than someone for whom it is a distraction.

Whatever the reason, you should be doing what you're best at even if you're not the immediate beneficiary of your effort. The new rule—let whoever does it best do it—is based on the need to integrate processes across corporate boundaries to reduce total effort, minimize total employed assets, and increase collective flexibility and responsiveness. "I win when you lose" is an increasingly naive notion. If you lose, we'll both end up holding the bag. If you're my customer and your costs go up, the decline of your market competitiveness will hurt me too. If you're my supplier and your costs go up, you won't be long for the world if that's not reflected in your price to me.

Recognizing that you have a self-interest in seeing that your customers and suppliers remain competitive doesn't mean sacrificing yourself on the altar for them. It does mean considering them not as adversaries, but as allies. It means working closely with them so that you all end up ahead. It means coordinating work across corporate boundaries, eliminating unproductive work by avoiding duplication. If I'm checking quality and we trust each other, why should you also check quality? Access to my quality control data may well be sufficient for you. Exchanging work—doing what you're best at, not everything you need—is not a demonstration of affection, altruism, or self-abnegation. The motivation is mutual self-interest. There is nothing inherently wrong with autarkic, self-contained companies. Producing narrowly defined products or services would be fine if it paid, but it no longer does. What pays today is interconnection and interdependency.

Many sophisticated companies have long realized that the official price quoted by their suppliers for a product is often only a fraction of the total cost associated with that product. A customer incurs purchasing, receiving, storage, handling, and inventory financing costs over and above what it pays to a supplier. A rational customer should not fixate on product price but on "total system cost," the total cost incurred for the product whether paid internally or to a supplier. Unfortunately, the Balkanization of our organizations—both internally and with regard to external parties—has made this obvious leap a hard one to make. For instance, purchasing agents are traditionally judged on the prices they pay, not on the total costs the company incurs. There are many reasons for this, not the least of which is that in the absence of a process perspective the data needed to calculate the total costs is hard to come by. The purchasing agent is responsible for product price; financing costs are somebody else's problem. A process-centered company, in contrast, is concerned with overall process performance. Suppliers are judged not by the numbers on their price sheets but by the costs and benefits that accrue from doing business.

In this new context, being "easy to do business with" becomes an overriding goal. Lowering your costs but raising costs to your customers is counterproductive. As products and services become more commodity-like and indistinguishable, what differentiates you from your competitors increasingly comes down to how well, how quickly, and with what ease you can liberate your customers from their problems (and therefore from their money).

If you do more for them—using your flexibility to simplify their operations, thus adding more value—you stand out and get the business. Your goal is not to minimize your costs or lower your inventory, it is to minimize total costs and total inventories while decreasing total cycle time. All the players win when the process as a whole wins, and that means looking at your customers and suppliers as teammates.

The ultimate extension of this idea may be to find points of potential cooperation even with competitors. Everyone is painfully aware that competition is increasing not subsiding, but there's a difference between smart and stupid competition. Doing your competitor a bad turn by doing yourself a worse one is stupid. Banding together with competitors to create an industry-wide process that reduces costs and improves everyone's capabilities is smart. This is not to suggest that competitors become friends or allies, or that all antitrust legislation needs to be repealed. It does suggest reducing the scope of competition to the areas where it makes sense to compete, leaving opportunities for cooperation in the areas where competition is harmful to all.

The theme of this chapter is the notion that Jack Welch of GE calls "boundarylessness," the dissolution of all walls within and around a business—the functional walls separating departments, the external ones keeping companies apart from each other, and the horizontal ones (i.e., ceilings and floors) that create artificial boundaries between "workers" and "managers." We've looked at all of these. But there is one other kind of wall to consider, the wall that separates companies (or business units as they are often known) that are parts of the same larger corporation. The challenge here is how one enterprise can be created from a collection of fractious, independent components.

The multibusiness enterprise is, of course, nothing new. General Motors and DuPont assumed their current forms more than a half century ago. However, the multibusiness company really came of age during the last forty years with the expansion of the American economy in the postwar period. Companies that sold life insurance found themselves diversifying into property and casualty insurance, setting up new business units to handle these new products. Soap manufacturers saw opportunities to sell toothpaste, pain relievers, food products, and other consumer goods, and likewise founded new units to serve those markets.

Although the definition of a "strategic business unit" is often nebulous, you can usually recognize it when you see it. In most organizations a business unit is essentially a self-contained company dedicated to providing certain products and services to selected customers. Its distinction from other units may be based on customers, on products and services, or on both. A large bank will typically be divided into a retail bank, a wholesale bank, and a capital markets group, each of which provides different financial services to different kinds of customers. An insurance company may offer virtually the same products and services to customers in different parts of the country through business units serving distinct geographical areas. A consumer products company may have separate business units serving the same retailer customers but have each concerned with developing and manufacturing a different set of products.

Multicompany structures enable greater flexibility and market focus than would be found in a single monolithic unit that attempted to be all things to all customers. But an enterprise comprised of many business units is often afflicted by rampant interdivisional strife in addition to run-of-the-mill interfunctional conflict. As we have noted, many business units treat sibling units even worse than they treat competitors. This actually makes a kind of sense, or at least is comprehensible given the operative assumption that your unit can shine only when other units falter. After all, your unit *does* compete with others for corporate attention, resources, and capital. Your unit's leaders compete with leaders of other units for promotion into higher corporate offices. Thus the most direct and visceral competition—and therefore the fiercest—has often been with nominal sibling units within a corporation.

Process centering is now reorganizing many of these units along new lines. Departmental executives and vice presidents are giving way to process owners and coaches. But a larger question remains: How do process-centered business units fit together to create a process-centered corporation?

For the last thirty years or so executives at both business unit and corporate levels have been fairly obsessed with the centralization versus decentralization debate. Some have argued that all functional activities of constituent organizations should be centralized as much as possible in order to maximize consistency and gain economy of scale. Thus many corporations with distinct business units that produced different products for sale to the same customers had a centralized, shared sales force serving all those units and products. Others had separate sales and marketing organizations for each unit but shared centralized manufacturing at the corporate level. The opposite extreme allowed every ship to sail on its own bottom. This entailed as much decentralization as possible, devolving autonomy to enable business units to meet the specific needs of their markets as they best determined, thereby robbing them of the excuse of their failings being attributable to the inadequacy of some shared resource.

In my travels through the corporate world I've noticed that senior executives are never more indecisive than when I ask them whether they prefer centralization or decentralization. Top managers seem to be in a perpetual winter of discontent on this issue. When centralized they yearn for the flexibility and autonomy of decentralization. When decentralized they lament its inconsistency, excess costs, and lack of control. Many executives have the opportunity to complain about both, for their organizations seem condemned to a sort of Sisyphean pendulum that swings back and forth, retreating from each alternative as its inevitable shortcomings materialize.

But relief is at hand. The centralization-decentralization trade-off is becoming increasingly spurious. Today a knowing corporate executive pressed to choose between the two will say "both," meaning that business units can obtain many of the distinct advantages previously associated with each option, simultaneously enjoying the operating autonomy of having their own local resources while using shared databases and telecommunications networks to connect with each other and with a corporate oversight group that will enable local decisions to be made in a larger context. Whether this is called "virtual centralization," "coordinated decentralization," or some such other unwieldy term, the point is that modern technology has obviated the need to make this Hobson's choice.

However, a new choice must be made involving the relative advantages and disadvantages of what may be called standardization and diversity in the process-centered corporation.

Different business units will often have processes with essentially the same name and purpose. Texas Instruments performs order fulfillment in each of its semiconductor, defense, consumer, and computer industry businesses. It would have been absurd to imagine TI centralizing order fulfillment—the very notion of a single, gargantuan facility filling orders from around the world for integrated circuits, calculators, computer software, and cruise missiles is ludicrous. Even within each business unit TI's order fulfillment is not a centralized process. Each unit has multiple facilities—at sales offices, factories, and distribution centers—where order fulfillment is performed. But this doesn't indicate how many different order fulfillment processes TI ought to have. Should TI have a single order fulfillment process designed, managed, and improved by a single process owner who is located organizationally, if not physically, at the corporate level? Or should it have multiple order fulfillment processes, one for each unit, so that each of the businesses can operate in a unique way that better responds to its specific requirements? In other words, should order fulfillment be *standardized* across TI or should TI's constituent units be allowed to *diversify* by designing and executing their own versions?

Diversity's advantages are clear. A business unit allowed to go its own way can optimize a process to meet the singular needs of its products and customers. By staying close to its market it can ensure that the process remains tuned to its customers' changing needs. The standardization alternative brings to mind Ambrose Bierce's definition of a compromise as the resolution of a conflict that leaves all parties equally *dis*satisfied. In other words, a process imposed on all business units by a corporate-level process owner—whose standard design will inevitably meet everyone's unique needs imperfectly—may make some units feel they are missing opportunities to outperform their competition.

On the other hand, complete diversity also has real disadvantages. First of all, every process involves some management overhead. Every process requires a process owner, who in turn needs staff support, in order to design, manage, and measure the process on a continuing basis. Each process also needs documentation and training materials. Multiple versions of the process will produce multiple versions of these materials. Information systems pose an even more serious problem. Virtually every process needs a supporting computer system that mechanizes the performance of some of its tasks, serves as a source and a conduit for the information that must flow among process performers, and measures process performance. Diverse processes require different information systems, while a standardized, enterprise-wide process needs but one common system whose development and maintenance costs can be amortized across a much larger user base.

Perhaps more importantly, a common computer system guarantees that data from all processes at all sites can be aggregated at the corporate level. When, for example, different business units each have a different order fulfillment process supported by a different computer system, the sudden request for an integrated invoice from a customer who is served by several units can be a daunting and expensive challenge. A common information system is an important guarantee of business flexibility, one of our most critical goals. A common system also helps the corporate organization gauge the performance of the company as a whole rather than just each business unit on its own.

Highly diverse processes also tend to harden the boundaries between business units, partly by reducing the fungibility of personnel who, if trained in standardized processes, could readily transfer between units should the need arise. Distinct processes thus serve to cement the existing unit structure into place more firmly than is desirable, since the division of a corporation into units that is right for today may not be the right one for tomorrow.

Even the most apparently natural business unit structure may grow obsolete. Changing technology can create connections between previously unrelated products, as may shifts in customer preferences, government regulations, and other aspects of the business environment. Such changes may require the combination of business units or the reallocation of products and customers across them. These market-dictated changes are much more difficult to make when the business units in question have highly diverse processes.

Not surprisingly, companies have taken different approaches to the standardization versus diversity issue. For example, all of Progressive Insurance's business units employ a dozen or so processes that are standardized across the entire corporation, each of which has a single owner. Bob McMillan, the company's claims process leader, described how that works in chapter 9. For Progressive—whose business units serve such geographical markets as California, Ohio, Florida, and so on—this is a perfectly reasonable decision, not an arbitrary bureaucratic edict. After all, there is no intrinsic reason why the claim process in Florida should work differently from the one in Ohio. In such cases the advantages of standardization overwhelm those that might be obtained from diversity. Texas Instruments on the other hand has distinct order fulfillment processes for each of its businesses. Imposing a single standard process on businesses with such different customers and products would make a Procrustean bed feel like a backyard hammock. It would be absurd to say that orders for calculators from Wal-Mart should be filled in the same way as orders for cruise missiles from the Pentagon.

Locating all processes of various business units at the corporate level achieves corporate consistency at the price of inflexibility. Allowing each unit to design and manage its own processes in order to meet its particular needs often leads to a lack of harmony at the corporate level. But an almost infinite spectrum of compromises lies between these polar extremes. Some companies have chosen to make some of their processes diverse and others standard across business units. Market- and product-focused processes (such as order acquisition, product development, etc.) are usually among those allowed to vary, thereby more precisely meeting the special require- ments of different units. At the other end, "backroom" processes such as procurement and financial operations are often standardized for the entire corporation to lower cost and enable enterprise-wide integration.

Hewlett-Packard produces such diverse products as medical instrumentation, communications systems, and computer peripherals. Because of the variety of these products, HP's product development processes are significantly different across its major business groups, each of which operates with a great deal of autonomy. At the same time, HP's businesses do have significant commonalities that the company does wish to exploit. To that end, HP has created a Product Process Organization, whose role it is to enable cross-business lever- age in product development processes. For instance, this unit has worked with the businesses to identify needs and opportu- nities for data sharing, has helped formulate a common parts numbering system, and operates certain facilities that all the businesses jointly "own."

The pendulum's ceaseless swing between centralization and decentralization showed that neither was a very viable alter- native. In contrast, standardization and diversity are both attractive when appropriately matched to the various needs of a corporation's businesses. We suggest the following rule of thumb: Processes should be as standardized as marketplace requirements will allow so long as standardization does mini- mal damage to the particular needs of a business unit's cus- tomers. To the extent that its processes can be standardized with those of others without causing major inflexibility and restraint on optimization, it is all to the good. Obviously, evaluating the costs and benefits of flexibility involves substantial subjective judgment. Most business units, bestowing on themselves the debased adjective "unique," will almost always claim that they deserve to go their own way because they are different from all their peers. Wise corporate leaders will listen to such pleas but recognize the self-interest in them and decide in the enterprise's interest as a whole.

All this should suggest that a corporation cannot be a collection of armor-plated business units operating independently and held together only by integrated financial arrangements. The walls between units must fall like all others.

When business units have virtually nothing in common, when one makes specialty chemicals for electronics manufacturers while another sells toys to consumers through retailers, the corporation essentially plays the cameo role of a holding company, a bank, or a venture capital firm. Its primary added value lies in assembling the different units into a portfolio that balances their attributes (e.g., cyclical versus countercyclical businesses, or growth versus mature businesses).

But a realization is growing that simply joining two unrelated businesses under a single corporate umbrella does little or nothing to improve either's operational performance. The real motivation for wedding two business units should be to find ways of integrating them so that each performs better. Therefore, a multiunit enterprise's real value lies in its opportunities to manage processes across many units.

Modern organizations have learned that the notion of economy of scale has severe limits. With size come *dis*economies of scale. As organizations grow, multiple layers of administrative bureaucracy inevitably appear and it becomes difficult for any individual to have an overall understanding of what's going on. Breaking a large organization into several smaller ones avoids this problem, but at the possible price of inconsistency. Standardized process design and centralized process management can eliminate much of the overhead associated with traditional decentralization, ensuring a degree of consistency and uniformity previously achievable only by physical centralization.

Robert Frost wrote that good fences made good neighbors. That may have been true in agricultural New Hampshire but it is not true in corporate America. In any case, as Frost also wrote in the same poem, "Something there is that doesn't love a wall." Process centering is one of those "somethings." Porous walls, walls that barely exist at all, walls that can be easily moved as the occasion requires, are the kinds of walls that a modern corporation requires. A popular epithet for an outstanding performer is that he or she "walks through walls." It is far easier to do this when they aren't there in the first place.

CHAPTER 12

RETHINKING STRATEGY: YOU ARE WHAT YOU DO

WHEN THOSE of us who helped pioneer reengineering first began urging companies to recognize and redesign their business processes, we seriously underestimated the impact our ideas would have.

We knew that companies could dramatically improve their efficiency and quality by focusing on customers and the processes that create value for them. But we didn't realize that companies' processes would in fact come to be even more important than their products. We started out thinking that if we could improve their processes—how companies work—we could help them compete better in their chosen marketplaces. And now it turns out that processes are in fact determining the marketplaces in which the companies compete. There are even instances in which processes have become products.

This idea that "the process is the product" is reminiscent in some ways of Marshall McLuhan's famous pronouncement that "the medium is the message." McLuhan meant that the electronic media were fundamentally transforming society not only by shaping the *content* of the information that people received, but also by changing the *way* in which they perceived and used it. Focusing on processes in the 1990s is having a similarly complex, subtle, and important effect on businesses. Just as viewers in the 1950s began to see events through the "cool" lens of the television camera, organizations have begun to see the world through a process lens. This process-driven focus is revolutionizing the way they define themselves and how they develop their strategies for future growth and success.

To explain this important but unexpected shift, we need to summarize the history of strategy formulation. This will be brief and oversimplified, but it will help put the latest changes in context.

Corporate strategic planning has traditionally been a discipline based on forecasting and positioning. Its basic premise has been that if a company could predict which markets would be strong in the future, it could then achieve success by producing the goods and services that would be demanded by those markets. In the early 1980s, thanks to the work of Michael Porter of the Harvard Business School, the scope of strategic planning was expanded to include the idea that competitive factors in the marketplace should be considered by planners. And more recently Gary Hamel and C. K. Prahalad have added the concept that a company's existing strengths, or core competencies, should also be factors in formulating strategy.

But now process centering is turning the whole concept upside-down. Although it agrees with Hamel and Prahalad when they say that strategies for the future should take into account what a company already does well, it redefines the concept of "what a company does" to mean the processes it performs rather than the goods or services it produces. Citizen Watch Company illustrates this difference: What it *produces* are watches; what it *does* is make tiny machines.

Over the past forty years there have been three major stages in the history of strategic planning. The first might be called the era of *portfolio management*. Its underlying concept, as developed by the Boston Consulting Group and Arthur D. Little, was that a corporation is a holding company, managing a pool of capital to be allocated among its constituent businesses. The central question of strategy, then, was how this capital was to be allocated. Typically a business was assessed in terms of two factors: its attractiveness (as represented, for instance, by its potential for growth) and its strength (as represented, for example, by its current market share). Strong and attractive businesses deserved the greatest amounts of capital; weak and unattractive ones, the least.

The portfolio approach helped corporate executives decide where to place their bets in the boom years of the 1960s, but it suffered from one fundamental conceptual flaw: the assumption that execution was easy. The strategist's job was to uncover the best opportunities; exploiting them was considered routine work that could be left to others. Over time it became clear that this disregard for implementation was absurd. In reality, execution is at least as important as conception. Or as George M. C. Fisher, Kodak's CEO, puts it: "The difficulty is not knowing what to do. It's doing it."

Strategic planning's second stage was the era of *competitive strategy*. In his landmark book of that title, Michael Porter suggested that the competitive dynamics of an industry and an analysis of a company's ability to compete in it needed to have a major hand in shaping the firm's strategy. Porter offered a framework, which he called the "five forces," to help companies assess their competitive context, and he outlined how they could choose among several generic strategies such as cost leadership and customer focus. But while Porter's work was a revolutionary advance, it was often applied in very limited ways. Many companies used it exclusively for analysis; it gave top managers insight but not action plans. Moreover, the question of execution continued to be given short shrift. Competitive strategy might help you decide what to do, but not how to do it.

The third era, in whose latter stages we now find ourselves, might be called that of *core competencies,* after the term popularized by Hamel and Prahalad. The underlying notion here is that every company needs to identify "the things that it is particularly good at" and build its strategy around them. Thus Honda's strategy of building lawn mowers, motorcycles, and automobiles represents an exploitation of its core competence in motors. As on-target as this notion is, however, it is notoriously slippery to apply. Companies find it very hard to identify and exploit their competencies. This is where process centering joins the story.

By focusing on processes and defining a business in terms of how it works, the process-centered perspective leads to strategies that address not only the question "What should we do?" but also "Can we do it?"

Until now, strategy work has been primarily an exercise in positioning. The primary goal of a strategic study was to identify a promising approach to a promising market or industry. Whether a company could actually *perform* in those markets has been largely ignored. Or in the devastating words of Fred Musone of Morton International: "Strategy in big business has turned into finding the right business where poor performance can be offset by structural and positional advantages."

Strategy has even carried with it an unspoken contempt for operations. In the minds of many strategists, execution is lowly work, safely ignored by those engaged in the lofty pursuit of strategy. Process centering rejects this view. It is a fundamental principle of the process-centered organization that execution is key.

Every MBA knows the story about the company that failed because it thought of itself as being in the buggy-whip business when it should have seen itself in the transportation business. In fact this old chestnut entirely misses the point. Strategy is not primarily about markets, either the narrow market for buggy whips or the broader one for transportation. Indeed a company that made and sold whips was highly unlikely to be positioned for manufacturing automobiles. What would have enabled it to succeed in a world of internal combustion engines? The company that sold buggy whips should have asked itself what it *did* best, at what *processes* it excelled. Perhaps its real strength lay in its leather fabrication processes, or in its process of filling orders from a network of independent small manufacturers, or in its product development process. Its future was more likely to lie with leather gloves or bags than with metal chassis. What a company *does* is central to deciding what it is, and where and how it should compete.

Progressive Insurance, for example, originally focused on processes and their improvement as a defensive response. Progressive's objective was to cut costs in the face of growing competition and regulatory pressure on rates. By reengineering its claims adjustment process, it slashed the time required to process a collision claim from an average of thirty-six days to twelve, cut its expense ratio from 33 to 24 percent of premiums, and increased income per employee by 70 percent. These improvements helped Progressive withstand the pressures being brought to bear on it. But they did more than just give Progressive a competitive advantage in the high-risk insurance market where it had been operating. The new processes that Progressive developed—for underwriting, claims, sales, marketing, and more—provided the company with the tools it needed to become an effective competitor in the much larger market for standard and preferred risks, in which it had previously had no presence and no prospects of success. Progressive discovered that if it could settle claims faster and cheaper for bad drivers, it could do so just as well for average and good drivers, Process capability took on a strategic significance that allowed the company access to new markets and in effect led it to redefine its strategy.

A process perspective can also help a company make decisions about what it should *not* do. When developing a new disk drive that would be roughly one-eighth the size of conventional drives, Hewlett-Packard evaluated its own process skills and concluded that it lacked the ability to handle and assemble such small components. Rather than attempt to develop such a process, HP turned to Citizen Watch Company. Citizen's *products* didn't interest HP, but its *processes* did. "As we began to see Citizen's capabilities for miniaturization and automation and their rigor in putting in place processes," says Bruce F. Spenner, general manager of HP's disk memory division, "it became clear that Citizen was the partner we wanted."

Hewlett-Packard was looking through a "process lens" when it selected Citizen to be its strategic partner. And it was using the same lens when it examined its own capabilities and decided that its process skills were in making "larger things," as Spenner puts it. A process lens gives a different view of a company and its strategic strengths and weaknesses from the usual market and product lenses. From this perspective strength in a market is less interesting than strength in a process. Viewed through a process lens, Citizen wasn't a watch company but a company that was good at miniaturization—just what HP needed. Once again, HP was attracted by what Citizen *did*, not what it *sold*.

You can look at many things though a process lens: at your own company, at potential strategic alliance partners (as Hewlett-Packard did), and at new opportunities.

Using a process lens, Circuit City, the electronics retailer, came to see itself as a company with superior processes in such areas as inventory management and handling consumer credit applications. These were the processes on which the company's success as a retailer had been based. Facing a leveling of growth in its traditional business, Circuit City looked through this lens to find a business where its process superiority would give it a competitive advantage. It discovered the used car market, a business, like consumer electronics, in which inventory management was key to cost control and in which buyers often applied for credit. The company's CarMax subsidiary is now selling used cars with great success and is seen as a force that will transform the automobile industry.

American Airlines' CEO Robert Crandall observed that his company seemed unable to make money consistently in the volatile airline business, despite the fact that it had very good processes. So he turned these processes into products. For instance, American now sells its aircraft maintenance services to Midway Airlines and Challenge Air, a cargo carrier, and is aggressively seeking additional maintenance customers. The company's reservations process is also a money-maker.

The point of these examples is that, by looking through a process lens, companies are increasingly defining themselves by their processes rather than by their current markets or products and services. What, after all, *is* a company? Management turns over, employees come and go, products have ever shorter lifetimes. At the end of the day a company *is* the processes through which it creates value. These are the longest-lived aspects of the organization. As times change these processes can be deployed in different ways and in different markets. Identifying the processes at which a company excels is the key to determining opportunities for growth and expansion. In other words companies are what they do—or can do—best.

Fred Musone observes that it is a delusion for strategists to think that they can find a business that will consistently offer disproportionate returns. The advantages will disappear as soon as potential competitors recognize your success. The goal, he says, should be to find businesses where improved ways of doing work will take advantage of those who went there to hide. "The strategic problem of the nineties is how to have better capabilities, not how to compete with the capabilities you have."

There are many ways in which companies can fashion strategies based on their processes. The following list identifies six such approaches that can be employed individually or in various combinations. The risks and the potential rewards of these approaches increase as you go down the list.

- *Intensification:* improving processes to serve current customers better
- *Extension:* using strong processes to enter new markets
- *Augmentation:* expanding processes to provide additional services to current customers
- *Conversion:* taking a process that you perform well and performing it as a service for other companies
- *Innovation:* applying processes that you perform well to create and deliver different goods or services
- *Diversification:* creating new processes to deliver new goods or services

Intensification: This approach involves deciding which processes matter most in a company's current markets and then working to improve them. This is a strategy for succeeding in a company's existing markets and is often the original reason for embarking on a reengineering effort.

At Federal-Mogul executives recognized the critical importance of the sample development process. They saw that improvement there would have a disproportionately high impact on overall business performance, and so set a strategy to achieve a performance breakthrough. When it succeeded, the company achieved enormous market-share growth. AT&T's Global Business Communications Systems (GBCS) felt the same way—and reengineered order fulfillment in order to reduce costs and increase customer satisfaction.

The flip side of intensification is that a company may realize that it is not worthwhile to invest in—or perhaps even to perform—processes that have marginal impact on its customers or in which it has no particular expertise. Hewlett-Packard observed that it was not adept at making "smaller" things. Many companies have decided that they are not good at logistics management. Such processes are candidates for outsourcing. Here, too, the process perspective dominates. It is not businesses or functions that are being outsourced but second-tier processes.

At GE in the 1980s Jack Welch had a famous dictum that the company's businesses had to be number one or number two in their markets or they would be closed or sold. Today it is imperative that a company be number one or number two—world-class—in its *processes*. Those that are not are candidates for outsourcing. No company can afford the drag on its performance or the distraction to its management that poor processes represent.

Extension: Extension entails building on existing processes to reach out and serve new customers. A company with superior processes can extend their use into new markets.

Progressive Insurance, as we've seen, used its reengineered claims handling process to extend its automobile insurance business. It had traditionally flourished in the high-risk market, but with improved claims handling it was able to compete in the more demanding market of standard- and preferred-risk drivers.

Texas Instruments' semiconductor group reengineered its

order fulfillment process in response to market changes for integrated circuits. The old process was well-matched to the characteristics of the old market—customers who bought standard products, orders that could be filled from inventory. However, in the early 1990s TI saw growth in demand shift to "application specific" chips that were custom designed for individual customers. Holding these chips in inventory carries a huge risk, since there is no way to predict demand for them, and so TI was forced to reengineer its manufacturing and shipping processes. It reduced its cycle time by more than two-thirds, which eliminated the need to build up inventories. The new faster process helped TI move into new markets where it has thrived.

Augmentation: Augmentation allows a company to enhance the value it provides customers by extending the reach of its processes. This often involves integrating a company's processes with the processes of the customer, breaking down walls as we discussed in chapter 11. For example, Goodyear augmented its order fulfillment process by integrating it with Navistar's materials acquisition process. Goodyear no longer just delivers tires to Navistar's warehouse, Goodyear now *operates* that warehouse and moves the right tires to Navistar's production line at the right time. It has further augmented its capabilities by taking over the job of mounting and balancing the tires. Augmentation has both increased Goodyear's income from Navistar and reduced its own inventory costs.

Progressive Insurance has augmented its service to retail customers by integrating its price quotation process with the customer's buying process. The company's ads now promote a toll-free number that offers instant cost and coverage information—not only about Progressive but also its leading competitors in the caller's area. By augmenting its own processes and doing the customer's work—obtaining prices from competing carriers—Progressive establishes a relationship of service, value, and trust. The result is that even when Progressive's rates are slightly higher than a competitor's, callers often buy from Progressive.

Conversion: Conversion is a more radical strategy that transforms an internal process into a salable service. As we've mentioned, American Airlines, which excelled in aircraft maintenance, decided to sell the performance of this process to other airlines. It has also turned its pilot and flight attendant training processes into revenue generators.

Electric utility companies know how to operate power plants and to read meters. Some have started capitalizing on this by contracting to operate the cogeneration plants owned by former power customers and to read meters and provide billing services for other utility companies. Blue Cross of Massachusetts now sells to other companies the telemarketing services it developed to enroll corporate employees in its health care programs. IBM operates a contract manufacturing service that builds computers and components for rival computer makers—in effect, converting its manufacturing process into a product. L.L. Bean has converted its vaunted order-taking and customer service processes into a fee-based service by selling it to companies like AT&T.

With a conversion strategy a company runs the risk of selling its crown jewels: proprietary capabilities built with substantial investment. On the one hand, some consider it prudent to reduce that risk by not offering services to direct competitors. On the other hand, the risk may be worth taking. What a company earns and learns from selling a process to others can be reinvested in process improvements that will continue to keep it ahead of the competition.

Innovation: We use this term in a nonstandard way to describe the application of existing process skills to new products and services. Even if new products and services appear quite different from existing ones, it may be that they can be delivered with slight variations of existing processes—in which case the company can expect to do well with them. We mentioned that Circuit City manages its electronics inventory so well that it found a new use for these process skills by moving into used car sales. The differences between the products—consumer electronics and used cars—were less important than the similarities in the processes underlying them.

Similarly, H & R Block has done well in temporary services businesses because it had a strong process for recruiting and managing trained people for short duration assignments—something it had a lot of experience doing just before April 15.

Since new products and services are full of surprises, innovation involves somewhat higher risks than the strategies mentioned above. But by leveraging existing process strengths, innovation need not be a venture into the wholly unknown.

Diversification: Diversification creates new processes to support new products and services. This is the riskiest strategy of the six because it requires the greatest change in what a company does, namely in its processes. More than just finding new markets, diversification means creating new ways of working as well. This is a bad choice for a company that can't be sure that it has, or can develop, a process advantage over competitors.

Deere & Company, the farm equipment manufacturer, developed processes to sell and deliver financial services in order to provide its retail dealers with insurance. Later a John Deere subsidiary started offering these services to auto dealers, boat dealers, and recreational vehicle dealers. This was a diversification (new processes) followed by an extension (new markets).

For diversification to succeed a company must possess an asset that will enable its new processes to outperform those of established competitors. What made an equipment manufacturer believe it could succeed at financial services? The answer was its sturdy dealer network and a strong relationship and credibility with customers—assets that enabled John Deere to develop highly competitive processes for new markets.

Obviously these techniques don't cover all the possibilities for converting process capability into strategy. Nor do they provide a detailed procedure for doing so. However, they do suggest that the conventional approach to strategic planning can be, and is being, turned on its head.

Traditional techniques for formulating strategy normally first concentrate on identifying potentially attractive markets and businesses and then look at whether it is feasible or possible to enter them. A process-centered approach starts by generating possibilities of what a company might be able to do well. Then it looks to see which, if any, are worthy of implementation.

This new process-centered approach to strategic planning requires a new kind of thinking as well as a new kind of strategist. Traditionally, strategy planning has focused on collecting and processing prodigious amounts of data about various markets. Strategy consulting firms were relentless in their pursuit of MBAs with the right analytic talents and skills. Now strategy has become a more creative endeavor. The hardest part is not determining the truth about various strategic options but generating those options in the first place.

Perhaps the most startling notion that arises from process-centered planning is the suggestion that long-range forecasting is a waste of time. It is a fundamental tenet of traditional planning that the future can, and should be, predicted. The goal of the traditional strategist was to forecast future demand and to come up with a plan for meeting it. The assumption was that the best strategy came from the most accurate forecast of the future.

In our age of relentless change, however, it is becoming increasingly clear that the best strategy is not one that tries to divine the future but one that responds rapidly to the present. "There is little strategic impact to be had in building processes that try to predict customer demand," observes Fred Musone of Morton International. It is much more significant, although infinitely harder, to "design processes that respond quickly to what a customer actually wants."

GE's Jack Welch acknowledged as much when he dismantled most of his company's famed central planning organization. "We may be surprised," he said, "but we'll no longer be surprised that we are surprised."

Acquisition and divestiture are two other strategic notions that change in the process-centered era. When capabilities are seen as crucial factors to success, acquisition strategies should no longer be based just on profit, product, or technology. In the same way divestiture no longer necessarily means getting rid of a business unit. It could simply mean outsourcing some of the company's less-than-stellar processes.

With a process focus, market share ceases to be the measure of success it once was. Among other reasons, economies of scale are no longer the key mechanism for achieving cost advantage and other forms of marketplace leadership. Although it may still be an important goal, market share is no longer a reliable indicator of current performance or a predictor of future success. A company with large market share today will retain it tomorrow only if the market doesn't change—an extremely unlikely occurrence. In a world of breakneck technology development, it doesn't matter who had 90 percent of yesterday's market; doubters need only ask IBM.

The once-celebrated learning curve may also have become a hindrance rather than a benefit in the process-centered corporation. That convention implied an assumption that over long periods of time accumulated volume would translate into cost leadership—an equation that no longer holds. Many companies have learned that maintaining the same processes for extended periods contributes to systemic weakness if, in the meantime, competitors have introduced new processes with superior designs and performance. The costs and ingrained behavior patterns associated with long-standing modes of operation can actually be a *dis*advantage to a company. Bell Atlantic learned this when its existing process for connecting customers to long-distance carriers proved to be inferior to those of start-up competitors. Bell Atlantic's years of experience with its old process and massive investments in systems to support it offered no protection against a simpler, better process. In the new world of process-centered planning the venerable advice to "stick to your knitting" remains valid, but "knitting" now takes on a new meaning. It means process, not product or market.

As we said at the opening of this chapter, those of us privileged to witness the advent of the process-centered era were slow to recognize the extent and magnitude of the changes it would entail. By now, however, the evidence is clear. Not only daily operations but the very definition of a company and the heart of the executive agenda—strategy formulation—are being reinvented. This shift is neither prospective nor optional. The company that continues to define itself by the products it makes or the markets it serves will not survive very long when competing with companies that have made the shift to process-based thinking and process-based strategy. The masters of process will be the masters of the twenty-first century.

CHAPTER 13

THE PROCESS OF CHANGE

FORTUNE'S ISSUE of May 3, 1993, had personal significance for me because it included an excerpt from *Reengineering the Corporation*. However, that issue's most important article was its cover story, which cut to the heart of every company's most fundamental challenge: the ability to compete over the long run.

"Corporate Dinosaurs" described the now familiar story of how three once mighty companies—IBM, General Motors, and Sears—were floundering amidst changing market conditions over which they had lost control.

However, a *Fortune* cover story on the same three companies in 1983 would have called them giants, not dinosaurs. In 1983, these were the elite of American industry: admired, emulated, even revered. These companies are a memorable illustration of Fred Musone's chilling reminder that "every big failure used to be a great success."

In 1983, Sears dominated American retailing; that year its sales were ten times that of Wal-Mart's. In 1983, GM was riding high, with a near-record share of the U.S. auto market. Roaring back after the disruption of the OPEC oil embargo, the venerated leader of the Big Three—and, many believed, of American industry in general—"owned" virtually every segment of the North American market that its management believed worth owning.

That same year IBM wasn't merely the world's largest computer company—with a stock market value that rose as high as $81 billion, some $16 billion higher than its nearest rival, AT&T—many people were convinced it was the world's best company of any kind. It was an icon of business. Long before benchmarking became de rigeur, IBM's marketing, manufacturing, and management systems established the standards to which other companies, computer and noncomputer alike, compared their own.

The advantages these three companies had—in brand recognition, customer loyalty, and human resources as well as in cash, plants, and other hard assets—gave them a shield of virtual invincibility. A specialty niche competitor might nibble at the edges of Sears' markets, but the notion of confronting the giant head-on was considered absurd. Who then sitting in Sears' Chicago headquarters, atop the world's tallest building, noticed a tiny regional discount chain operating from Bentonville, Arkansas, and calling itself Wal-Mart? In 1983 Microsoft was a single-product vendor to IBM, one of thousands whose success seemed to hang on Big Blue's continued favor. And so long as mighty GM owned the high-end, high-margin market, who in Detroit worried about Toyota's awkward-looking econoboxes?

In some respects the contextual changes that confronted and confounded these giants of the 1980s were neither profound nor extraordinary. Drivers didn't give up cars. People didn't stop buying lawn mowers, clothes for their kids, or washing machines. The need for computing didn't suddenly diminish. Nor were these changes invisible or hatched in secret. Wal-Mart stores weren't open only at night when Sears executives were sleeping. Apple didn't disguise its PCs as toasters. Nissan and Honda didn't affix Chrysler and Ford nameplates to their cars to fool GM scouts. GM, Sears, and IBM saw the changes in their environment. It was impossible not to. Their leaders even thought they were responding to them—but they weren't. Even when it became obvious that they avoided changing at their peril, they did not act; indeed, it seems that they *could* not act.

Their paralysis underlines a profound lesson that companies must learn from the whole of the last, turbulent decade: Responding to change, like any other business activity, requires the right mechanisms and processes. It does not happen automatically.

Eventually these three lagging giants got around to making—or at least to starting to make—major changes, but not until they had come perilously near the brink (and their senior executives had been swept from office). Why didn't they do these things earlier? The answer is actually simple. They didn't because they couldn't, and they couldn't because they had no organized means of doing so. These companies, like most others, were not designed to change.

The trouble was that companies designed to the model born of the Industrial Age were built with far more emphasis on ensuring continuity than on enabling basic change. Marginal changes were of course possible. Successful companies were accomplished in product evolution and variation. Costs could be incrementally reduced. Businesses could be acquired or sold. However, most companies were—and remain—incapable of making fundamental changes, breaking their existing frameworks. Most aren't even aware of these frameworks, although they govern everything the companies do. The assumptions built into a company's structure and culture may be as invisible as an aquarium's glass walls, but they nonetheless define the limits of action and exploration for the people within.

Indeed, we can go further and say that most organizations were designed *not* to change. They were organized and managed with the implicit belief that basic change does not happen, that the future of the organization is largely the same as its past, that the goal of management is merely to maintain and perfect the model devised by the company's long-departed founder.

There are many subtle and not so subtle ways in which the existence of change is denied and responding to it is impeded. Hierarchical organizational structures create fragmented perspectives, so that no one near the front lines can see enough of the big picture to recognize that fundamental change is happening in the environment—while the people at the top are too far removed to notice much of anything.

When a new idea is conceived in a traditional company without built-in change enabling mechanisms, it must run a gauntlet of gatekeepers before reaching anyone with the authority and resources to act on it. Even when a good idea manages to find a champion, it is analyzed and pondered by a seemingly endless parade of task forces, committees, and study groups. By the time the notion gets to a point of action the opportunity it was meant to capture has often passed. The implicit assumption underlying all this is that innovation is risky and suspect, and that carrying on in the traditional way is almost always the best course. Is it any surprise, therefore, that major product innovations rarely come from the established leaders in the industry? IBM did not lead the minicomputer or the PC revolution, Merck did not pioneer biotechnology, and while RCA invented the VCR, it soon abandoned it to the Japanese. The institutional forces of the large organization are innovation killers. It is only the rare company, like 3M, that has managed not to submerge its entrepreneurial antecedents.

Stable, predictable business conditions fostered a style of planning that was almost Soviet in its rigidity. "Strategic plans" were often little more than straight-line extrapolations of the past into the future. The underlying mind-set was that major change was a millennial phenomenon that had last manifested itself long ago at the company's founding, and that now could safely be assumed to have run its course. Plans would be created in April of one year with objectives set for the following one. They were then followed like Holy Writ; falling short of a plan was a cardinal business sin. This may have worked in the 1960s, but the assumption that anything can be reliably forecast fifteen to twenty months hence is now absurd.

Most companies' compensation systems were also designed to reinforce and perpetuate behavior inimical to change. When employees are paid for putting in time, time—not creativity—is what employers can expect from them. When incentive plans reward success but ignore or punish worthy failure, even the boldest innovators will limit themselves to sure bets that will be equally obvious to the competition.

The cultural values embedded in most organizations celebrated precision. An aspiring manager made a good impression with exactitude, not hunches. Few people would ever say "I don't know," even when it was true. Senior managers were rarely interested in hearing about ideas that "might" work. A fantasy world of decision trees and Bayesian analysis perpetuated a mind-set that the world was predictable, and that failure, a sign of incompetence, was avoidable.

There were exceptions to this picture, of course. Some companies did *occasionally* react quickly to outside events. But it is instructive to observe how they did so. I once visited a major electronics company that had departed successfully from its long-held strategy and captured an emerging market well before the competition. How did this company manage to move so fast? A member of the corporate executive committee had overheard something interesting in a ski resort's lift line. He jotted a note, which somehow did not get lost, and raised the issue at the next executive committee meeting, where it struck a chord with a number of other senior managers. From there it was easy. In short, this innovation was a fluke, a matter of luck, rather than a deliberate outcome of an organized system. But you can't count on being lucky, and flukes do nothing to assure a continuing organizational responsiveness to change.

Indeed, a formal system for change is not even on most companies' radar screens. An analogy to the 1950s presents itself. A visitor to a typical company in that decade who inquired into that company's strategic planning system would have been greeted with blank stares. "We make it and sell it and don't need fancy planning systems" was a common sentiment of the day. Such companies learned in the decades to follow of their need for strategic planning. Today an inquiry into a company's systems for change will provoke similar scorn. Yet a company without a system for change is not likely to change. And although it appears on no balance sheet, a systemic and institutional capacity for change may now be a company's single most valuable asset. What allowed Wal-Mart to confront Sears and succeed? Consumers might say it was low prices and good service. Suppliers and competitors might say it was Wal-Mart's cultivated ability to buy for less and its now famous logistics systems. Sam Walton, however, had a different view. In one of his last interviews Wal-Mart's founder and guiding genius asserted that he felt his company vanquished the competition because it was better at making changes. At their now legendary Saturday morning meetings Wal-Mart senior managers from around the country gather to review what did and didn't work that week. They decide right then and there what to do about it and proceed to make it happen. Wal-Mart never allows itself to become prisoner to an accepted way of doing things. This capacity for change, which is the real hallmark of Wal-Mart's operation, is an absolute necessity for survival and growth in today's world.

Hewlett-Packard appreciates the need to institutionalize a capacity for change. Its competitors—Digital and Wang, for example—did not. Presumably because its headquarters are near California's vineyards, HP executives often use wine metaphors in conversation. In particular, each of their products is assigned a "vintage," the year in which it is introduced. Lately, more than 75 percent of HP's revenues are from products whose vintage is three years old or less, and this percentage is growing. Hewlett-Packard has recognized that in such an environment it cannot afford to be the company it was five years ago.

One of the most widely covered business news stories of 1993 was the contest between Viacom and QVC to acquire Paramount and thereby achieve control of the emerging information superhighway. If that story had been published in 1988, readers would have wondered what QVC and Viacom were and would have tried in vain to imagine what on earth an information superhighway was. This phenomenon is not limited to the entertainment industry. Almost every established company, large or small, currently faces crises that would have seemed absurd or incomprehensible five years ago. Competition in the electric power industry? To traditional electric-power executives, "marketing" meant going to the grocery store. The once proud pharmaceutical industry is trying desperately to envision its future in a world of managed care. Everyone is frantically checking their balance sheets for exposure to derivatives. Retailers are staring anxiously at empty malls, "dress down" days at the office, and the prospect of commerce on the Internet. Things ain't what they used to be—if they ever were.

Do these crises represent, as some people charge, a failure

of strategic planning? Should power industry executives and pharmaceutical leaders be faulted for failure to foresee today's reality, which was yesterday's future? I think not. Strategic planning is a valuable tool for extrapolating well-established, long-running trends. It's useful for preparing for the expectable future. But the kinds of changes companies are experiencing now are unexpected and unanticipatable. The pace of change has accelerated; the time horizon has been foreshortened. By the time companies can sight an approaching change its effects are already upon them. By the time most companies work out what's going to happen, it already has.

Will the business agenda for 1996 also be the business agenda for 2006? *No one knows.* Those who say they do know are fools or charlatans. The next decade will see change every bit as mind-boggling and ornery as has the last one. The old business version of Newton's first law of motion—that a company that did a billion dollars last year will do more or less a billion this year—has been repealed. The rate of change in the economic environment has become exponential. Organizations built for yesterday can't and don't work today, and today's organizations may not work tomorrow.

Then what on earth should be done? How can companies prepare to meet the business issues of the next decade if they're unpredictable? The answer is that they can accommodate the forces of change only by creating and institutionalizing a capacity for changing themselves. The secret of success is not predicting the future; it is creating an organization that will thrive in a future that cannot be predicted.

But what does it mean to institutionalize a capacity for change? Speeches and noble slogans are not enough—they're not even close. The solution to this conundrum is for the company to treat its need for change as seriously as it treats its "real" work—the value-creating activities that most people consider the heart of their business.

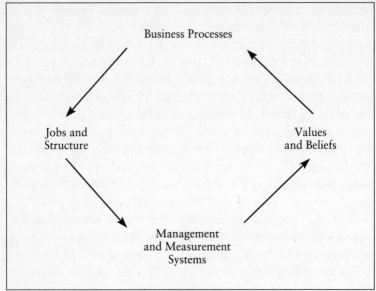

Figure 4

Reengineering the Corporation introduced the "business diamond," depicted in Figure 4, to express the fact that every organization can be described in terms of four major features: its business processes, its jobs and organizational structure, its management and measurement systems, and its values and beliefs. The design of the company's business processes determines the nature of people's jobs and the ways in which they are organized to perform that work. The nature of jobs and the organization of work, in turn, determine the kinds of management systems a company must establish and use. These management systems, such as performance measurement and employee compensation, shape the values and beliefs held by employees—that is, what they consider to be important in their work. And, finally, employee values and beliefs must be consistent with and support the design of the company's business processes, the top point on the business diamond.

The entity described by the business diamond—processes, jobs and organization, management and measurement, and values—is both vital and visible. It's what customers, employees, and managers see and respond to. It is the *system* that delivers today's products or services. However, that system must also deliver tomorrow's products or services, which might be—almost certainly *will* be—substantially different from today's. Just as marketing and manufacturing in the 1990s differ from their antecedents in the 1950s, current processes will surely be inappropriate for the demands to come during the next five years. And as these processes change, so must all the other facets of the diamond. In other words, a company's business system, incorporating the diamond's four linked points, is neither fixed nor permanent. It must change as the demands upon it change.

But how can it? People living and working in a business system cannot change it. Their perspectives are foreshortened, their information gathering and measurement systems reinforce the past, and their incentives encourage continuity. Archimedes proclaimed, "Give me where to stand, and I will move the earth." But where should those who might change a business system be standing?

The answer is that every organization needs *two* business systems. Borrowing a term from linguistics, we shall call them the *surface* system and the *deep* system. Thus far we have focused on the surface system. It is comprised of the organized tasks of the business processes, with their attendant jobs, structures, systems, and values. But this surface system is in periodic need of major change. Accomplishing that change is the job of the deep system.

The deep system creates no customer value; it makes no products and delivers no services. It doesn't process orders, develop new products, or create value for customers. Rather it monitors, governs, adjusts, and reforms the surface system that does create customer value. A company's deep system bears the responsibility for detecting external changes, determining what those changes mean, and intervening to modify or transform the surface system accordingly. The deep system, working beneath the surface, embodies the capacity to change.

The deep system continually hurls challenges: Is this still the right way or the best way to do things? If not, what is? The deep system ensures that the appropriate internal change—moderate or radical—takes place, shaping and reshaping the organization to take account of, and whenever possible take advantage of, ongoing external change.

The Romans, it is said, had a custom that ensured victorious leaders did not lose their sense of proportion. As a successful general was led in triumph through Roman streets lined with adoring crowds, a man stationed behind him would continually whisper in the general's ear: "Remember that you are mortal." The general is the surface system, and the man whispering the truth is the deep system.

A deep system must be more than a vague management desire to keep the company's value-creating processes up to date. Like the surface system, it must consist of specific processes with supporting jobs and organizational structure. It also has its own management and measurement mechanisms that foster specific values and beliefs.

In other words, the deep system is real and concrete, not an abstract philosophy. The primary processes of the deep system are three: learning, redesign, and transition. Their cumulative output is surface system change. As with the surface system's more familiar processes, the deep system processes can work effectively only if they have design and owners, organized execution, and rigorous management.

By means of the learning process the need for major change to the surface system is recognized, communicated, and accepted. This process identifies important information and then ensures that it is understood, evaluated, and spread through the organization. Its specific output is the decision to change and concrete objectives for this change. Most companies unconsciously perform this process in bits and pieces—conducting, for example, strategic market intelligence, competitor analysis, or technological forecasting.

But gathering information through formal mechanisms such as benchmarking and specialized staff such as competitive analysts is just a part of what must be a much broader and inclusive process. Information must be gathered from everyone in the organization, especially from frontline employees, who are best equipped to recognize inadequacies in current operations or significant changes in customer needs. To say that the deep system has an independent identity and existence is *not at all* to say that it is performed by deep system specialists who reside in a deep system department. There would be no more certain guarantee of its failure. Everyone in the company must live simultaneously in the surface and deep systems, simultaneously performing today's work and reflecting on it.

However, learning involves more than the acquisition of knowledge and information. It also requires discussion and debate, the crucible in which flashes of insight are born and developed. It must include mechanisms to ensure a fair examination of ideas that appear outrageous and unacceptable at first glance.

The learning process can in fact be described in terms of two subprocesses. The first is exploration. Traditional organizations tend to look only at conveniently found information, most of which is collected by surface systems as part of their job. Unfortunately, this information tends to reinforce the surface system, not shake it up. Measures of consumer preference would do little to help a brand manager realize that the name of the game was now retailer preference and that lousy distribution processes would quickly cause a loss in shelf space—no matter what consumers thought. We need information that comes from out of the box if we are to recognize the box's limitations. The key questions are the ones you never thought to ask before, and the most important information is that which you don't have and never thought you'd need. By definition, major change is always a surprise, and looking for it in all the old familiar places is a colossal waste of time. The deep system's exploration subprocess must search beyond the obvious to find information overlooked by, hidden from, or even hidden by the surface system.

Interpretation is the other learning subprocess: analyzing, debating, and deciding on the meaning of the collected information. The broadest possible perspectives must be brought to bear on the information. Many different kinds of people must engage in this debate, both for what they have to offer and to gain the widest possible acceptance for the outcome.

Redesign, the second deep system process, takes the output of the learning process as its input and creates a new design for the surface system that better fits the new external realities. Old surface processes and their supporting mechanisms are reconsidered, and better ways of doing them are devised.

Transition is the deep system process by which the organization's old surface system is replaced by a new one. It takes as input a new surface system design, and its result is the new system in actual operation. The transition process encompasses such disciplines as change management and implementation. It is concerned with translating ideas into realities.

These three deep system processes are more than names for a willingness to learn and change. They are concrete processes that real people perform and for which real people hold real responsibility. Together they comprise the heart of what is coming to be called a "learning organization." That term, however, is inadequate, since learning alone is insufficient. It is but the first of three essential deep system processes. To quote the Talmud, "Study is not of the essence, but rather action." Learning without design and transition is a solipsistic waste of time.

To summarize: Learning decides to create new ways of working, redesign invents those new ways, and transition installs them. These processes are sometimes found in organizations, but generally in a haphazard and inadvertent condition. When companies organize learning, redesign, and transition as deliberate processes no less real than those in the surface system, then change becomes purposeful, deliberate, and amenable to control. In effect, the three deep system processes accomplish what we have called reengineering, and embedding them in a system institutionalizes the capacity to reengineer—to respond as needed to ongoing change.

As we've mentioned, the deep system is not a self-contained unit, something apart and separate from the rest of the company. Everyone in the company, whatever his or her surface system job, also works in the three deep system processes.

Process owners live half in the surface system (supporting the operation of the current process) and half in the deep system (ensuring that it changes when necessary). Moreover, as process performers do the "real" work of surface system processes—developing products, serving customers, shipping orders—they simultaneously participate in the "meta-work" of the deep system processes. For instance, the sales rep in the field, ever alert to changes in customer needs, must understand that any information he or she happens to learn in the course of a sales call is vitally important, but has no value if it remains locked in the car trunk. As participants in the deep system learning process, sales reps must know how and with whom to share their knowledge. So must the technician on the manufacturing line who comes up with a new idea or recognizes a flaw in the existing method of manufacturing.

Please note: Installing an employee suggestion box is *not* creating a deep system learning process. People with new information—which is to say everyone in a company—must do more than pass it on. The learning process includes acquiring information and ideas from employees, but it entails far more as well—obtaining potentially relevant information from external sources and from the firm's own systems; analyzing, discussing, and debating the meaning of information; creating scenarios about its implications; and reaching a conclusion as to how to proceed. The same frontline personnel who offer the original data must participate in the interpretation as well. *That* is process. A suggestion box is empty tokenism.

While everyone in the organization will contribute to the deep system processes, some people will work exclusively, or at least primarily, in one or more of them. For lack of a better term we will call them reengineers, makers of and experts at change, which is what the deep system is all about. Since external change is now a permanent condition rather than an occasional event, organizations must develop a cadre of experts highly proficient in its three critical processes.

The learning process requires people who are adept at identifying unprecedented trends in multidimensional data and have an intuitive sense for extracting coherent trends from conflicting data (the role that physicists are now playing in stock market analysis—separating the signal from the noise). The design process puts a premium on creative individuals with a capability for thinking out of the box, identifying and rejecting received assumptions, and recognizing how new technology rewrites the rules of business. The transition process requires change agents, people effective at influencing opinions and attitudes so as to persuade fellow employees to release the familiar and embrace the uncertain. These skills are real, concrete, and specific, and it is far from impossible to find people who possess them (although they tend to be accidental rather than deliberate products of our educational system). What is most striking is how undervalued these skills have been in our organizations to date. We have favored people good at executing plans, not those good at raising troubling questions or good at answering them.

We must recognize that some people have a special skill at bringing about change just as others excel in doing and performing in existing formats. Just as we need sales reps, engineers, and finance experts in our organizations, we need change makers as well. The crisis of change will never pass. Without changers in an organization, the doers will remain forever stuck in what they're doing today.

But finding reengineers today is like looking for computer programmers in the late 1950s. There's no recognized cadre of such people, no established professional school to produce them, and no particular college degree they're likely to claim. Just like programmers several decades ago, they are as likely to have degrees in music and philosophy as in administration or finance.

Rather than looking for credentials alone, companies are likely to find change agents by seeking people with talents and characteristics that mark them as potential reengineers. Chief among these are an almost organic dissatisfaction with the status quo, a creative itch to improve things, and an ability to see processes and businesses holistically. Although they are not immune to power, money, or glory, that's not what primarily makes them tick. Bored by routine, they're energized and animated by challenge. They are always looking for a higher mountain to scale, a bigger wave to ride. Of course they must be able to work within a corporate context, but it's equally important that the corporate context be able to include them.

The three deep system processes—learning, redesign, and transition—need owners just as much as any surface system process. *Reengineering the Corporation* called their owner the reengineering czar. Here we'll use the term CTO: Chief Transformation Officer. "Reengineering czar" has too much of a short-term project emphasis. As we've seen, the role and responsibilities it discharges must be permanent fixtures of the organization. Whether or not the CTO title catches on, the role is starting to. The CTO is both the leader of a company's change agents and reengineers and the owner of the principal change processes.

The CTO is analogous to a CFO. Every modern manager needs some appreciation of finance; it is not the CFO's job to perform all of a company's financial transactions. Rather, the CFO ensures that the organization's financial assets are managed effectively as a whole. Similarly, the CTO doesn't effect all the changes in a company but rather ensures that the deep system processes are being performed well by people throughout the organization. The processes themselves are part of everyone's job; managing them is the CTO's responsibility. Ongoing change is everybody's business but it is the CTO's profession.

As we've said, the deep system, like the surface system it constantly adjusts, entails a complete four-pointed business diamond. As above, so below, to paraphrase Galileo. The design of the company's deep system processes determines the nature of the jobs people perform in those processes and the ways in which they are organized to perform the work. This in turn shapes a set of management and measurement systems and from thence a set of values. Once again, this complete system coexists with but is independent of the currently reigning surface system. Thus deep system processes require that people be measured for what they've learned, not just for results achieved in the surface system. If only today's performance is measured, people will never invest time in finding the ideas and acquiring the skills that will determine tomorrow's. Likewise, a system that rewards only successful results encourages people to limit themselves to trying sure bets, an approach ludicrously insufficient in a world of change. A change-oriented company will measure and reward learning, risk-taking, and progress toward change in order to reinforce and encourage the deep system processes. If companies don't make every employee's participation in deep system processes an explicit part of their evaluation, deep system processes will get little energy or attention.

The management systems that support deep system processes must also include recruiting and development practices that seek, value, and recognize the particular characteristics required for change agents. Reengineers can't afford to wear narrowly focused lenses. On the contrary, they must demonstrate a wide breadth of perspective. Their backgrounds must be varied enough to ensure multiple points of view. Therefore, the deep system management systems must accommodate and encourage short-tenure jobs and extensive job rotation in order to develop well-rounded change agents. Such job rotation is part of a reengineer's life-long learning—not a luxury in a time of relentless change but an instrument of survival. Indeed, such systems should also be applied to everyone in the organization, not just to reengineers, so that all frontline personnel have the broad perspective that will help them recognize change, accept it, and decide what to do about it.

Management communication systems must also change to encourage learning. Traditionally, communications were channeled vertically, up and down the organizational hierarchy, with dissemination based on the "need to know" principle. Deep system processes demand omnidirectional communication channels that operate on the principle of "might be interesting to know" or "when in doubt, let it out." The deep system processes, especially learning and redesign, can thrive only in an information-rich environment. As in a research lab, the sharing of new, immature, untested ideas is a prerequisite for creativity and innovation.

The fourth point of the business diamond—values and beliefs—demonstrates a crucial difference between surface and deep systems. Surface system values change over time, even those that *appear* to be inviolable, such as "the customer comes first." The customer doesn't come first in a quasi-monopoly environment like that of the post–World War II decades. Putting the customer first is today's conventional wisdom only because it has pragmatic economic value in today's economic environment. In other words, a company's surface system should value placing the customer first when doing so makes good sense. When it doesn't, it shouldn't. The fact that a surface system value may have only temporary validity should not, however, diminish the intensity and passion with which it is held. If a value is right for the times, the organization must commit to it deeply and completely. The organization must, however, accept the notion that this value may be replaced by another in the future.

But deep system values do not change. These values do not support any particular surface system; rather they support change itself. Self-examination and self-criticism are the prime deep system values. Arrogance, narrowness, and complacency are the natural enemies of organizational adaptation and evolution. A company that holds itself to be invincibly excellent is an organization that will soon become the captive—and then the victim—of its currently reigning surface system. Energetic and talented change agents, a powerful CTO, and on-the-mark performance measurement systems aren't enough to overcome the paralysis born of conceit. "Remember, all glory is fleeting," warns Fred Musone, sounding very much like the Roman general's sidekick. "Don't take yourself too seriously. To me, that's the characteristic of a long-term successful company: humility." If the deep system values of the organization don't include that humility, the deep system processes simply won't work.

A restless curiosity and probing inquisitiveness must also be highly valued in the deep system diamond. Naturally, these qualities will provoke discomfort and disagreement, but the alternative serenity breeds deadly torpor. The Hegelian dialectic—the clash of thesis and antithesis resolving into a new synthesis—must be allowed free play. If change is indeed a constant condition then the ability to keep pace with that change will require a vigilance, intelligence, and diligence never before required of more than a few. Now, and for as far forward as we can see, success will belong to the most restless and most alert.

PART IV

SOCIETY

CHAPTER 14

WHAT I TELL MY CHILDREN

MY CHILDREN are in their high school and college years. I have often wondered how best to advise them to find their ways in a process-centered world. Should they regard their futures with anticipation or dread? How can they best prepare themselves? What will it take to fashion a successful business career in this new world? In so doing, I am drawn to Dickens' description of the 1790s as "the best of times, the worst of times." We need look no further for a capsule description of the present. The 1790s were the worst of times for French aristocrats—functionaries of the *ancien régime*—whose destiny was the guillotine; it was the best of times for the *philosophes*—the thinkers of the Enlightenment—who had defined the principles of the new society being created in front of their eyes. Today is the worst of times for corporate aristocrats who, like French nobles, think that their "status" should assure their future. They too are headed for a corporate guillotine. But it is the best of times, a paradise of possibilities, for those who embrace change and grasp its opportunities.

We are, to use Auden's phrase, in a new Age of Anxiety. People can't play by the old rules anymore. They recognize this fact, but they aren't clear what the new rules are. Everyone is searching for verities and certainties, for surefire formulas for surviving in a new environment. The bookstores are awash with career advice. Twenty dollars will buy *The Complete Career Guide for the 21st Century* or *The Secrets of Success*, claiming to identify the hot careers, the best locations, the right education, all the requisites for personal success.

I make no such pretenses. It would be overreaching and self-contradictory for me, having just argued that the process-centered world is replete with peril and uncertainty, to offer my children (or anyone else) a foolproof recipe for success. I offer instead a perspective, together with some modest suggestions, on successful business careers in this world. Even this I offer hesitantly and with reservations. Walter Mondale said in a presidential debate, "Mr. Reagan will raise taxes. So will I. He won't tell you. I just did." I want to be as forthright. Neither I nor the authors of the surefire guides to success know what the world will look like in ten years; the difference is that I admit it.

An idea we must immediately dispense with is that there is a single winning career path for the twenty-first century. Modern experience quickly disabuses us of such notions. For much of this century, medicine, law, and investment banking were virtually sure-fire paths to prosperity and possibly to glory; that is no longer the case. Health care is in a state of transition, to put it mildly; many lawyers are tending bar instead of serving at it; and bankers are being merged out of business.

With the same certainty that Benjamin in *The Graduate* was urged to pursue plastics, today's career guides tout software and biotech. These career choices of the moment may be good for 1996, but will they still be good in 2006? A breakthrough in software technology could readily saturate the "inexhaustible" demand for programmers. Changes in healthcare funding will alter the nature of medical research and the skills it requires. No one knows which careers offer a secure and predictable future—or whether any will. Achieving success is too complex for simple nostrums.

First, some good news. Personal success in the process-centered world is still open to rational pursuit. Some people suggest that life after reengineering is "nasty, brutish, and short"—that global competition, demanding customers, and mobile capital will conspire to produce ever fewer jobs and an environment in which employees can barely keep their heads above water. This is nonsense.

No one denies that the transition to process centering has accounted for layoffs and severe dislocations. But this is temporary. The point of reengineering is not the elimination of jobs; it is the elimination of non-value-added work. As this work disappears, jobs often go along with it, transforming the organization into a leaner and more efficient enterprise. But what happens next? Only hopelessly unimaginative companies will remain in their newly reduced circumstances. The rule for business enterprises, as for all forms of life, is to grow or die. And as new efficiencies make them more competitive, they will grow and add jobs. Progressive Insurance is again a case in point. In 1991 the company had approximately 7,600 employees and $1.3 billion in revenues. A year later, after intense reengineering, the company was down to 6,000 employees with $1.45 billion in revenue. By 1995 their lower cost structure and better customer service allowed them to grow to $3 billion and add 2,000 new jobs, for a total of 8,000. Leaner and meaner had become bigger and better.

Process centering allows companies to achieve unprecedented improvements in productivity that will in turn lead to more jobs and higher standards of living. Indeed, the only route to increased prosperity is through such temporarily disruptive breakthroughs in productivity. If everyone is busy making cars and refrigerators, who is available to make VCRs? Admittedly, the shift from cars to VCRs can be tough on the autoworkers, but in the aggregate we come out way ahead. Process centering will repeat the history of all major advances of the last two hundred years: a brief period of dislocation followed by a new plateau of greater prosperity. New and previously unanticipated desires and demands always arise to soak up the surplus labor pool created by increased efficiency at producing the old goods and services. Unless one believes that the human race will suddenly deny its desires and decrease consumption in order to adopt a simpler and ascetic way of life, process centering will be merely the latest in a long series of job-creating, not job-destroying, innovations.

This does not mean that the process-centered world is without problems. Any major change produces winners and losers. The trick is to understand the difference between the two and take steps to make sure you are in the right column, ready to take advantage of the opportunities.

Now for some bad news. Success will not be a simple matter of picking the right career and the right company to work for. Success in the process-centered world will come from within, not from without. It will not be based on what you do but on who you really are. Success begins by determining whether you are the kind of person with the stuff of success— and if you are not, transforming yourself into someone who is. This is the basic premise that must be kept in mind by the student as well as by the anxious middle-aged job seeker and by the manager trying to reposition himself or herself in a newly process-centered company.

The Reengineering Revolution cited the president of a small company who said that reengineering had changed his hiring criteria. Formerly, he had hired on "skills and salary," selecting

the least expensive people with the skills required for the particular job. Now he hires on "attitude and aptitude," finding people who can learn the skills required for the job and who will
then perform it with spirit, enthusiasm, and self-reliance. In the
same spirit I suggest that there are two key ingredients to personal success in the process-centered environment: cognition
and character, the ability to think and the right set of attitudes.

A factory worker at a process-centered pharmaceutical firm
recently described what the company's shift has meant to him:
"I no longer have to check my brain at the gate." Thinking
was not a requisite for most traditional jobs. Blue-collar
workers were expected to follow orders, not to think. They
had narrow tasks to perform, designed to be as "idiot-proof"
as possible. Even white-collar workers, who presumably used
their minds more than their hands, had tight limits on the use
of their brains. An engineer was expected to think about engineering, not about sales or service. Similarly, sales and service
reps were expected to stick to their narrow functions.
Certainly, no "worker" was to consider the big picture, how
his or her work related to the work of others or how it led to
customer satisfaction and company success. Such concerns
were the exclusive domain of "management." No longer.

A traditional order handler followed a preprogrammed set
of rules to allocate inventory and schedule shipments. Now a
process-oriented order handler takes into consideration the
different competitive situations of different customers, likely
delivery times from suppliers on out-of-stock items, the availability of trucks at the shipping dock, and myriad other factors. The results: better use of inventory, happier customers,
and lower shipping costs. To achieve these results, the order
processor must be able to comprehend and deal with the
process as a whole, not just with its individual tasks. This
kind of cognitive capability has not historically been much in
demand. It is even as novel to most university graduates as it
is to high-school graduates.

The essence of this new cognitive style is the ability to see how parts connect, how numerous individual pieces add up to a totality, and how each affects the whole. It means visualizing and understanding a complex system. It also means having an intuition, a gut feel, for a system so that decisions can be made in the face of ambiguity and incomplete information. The decisions that the order handler has to make are not open to mathematical analysis and formal optimization; they require a feel for the process and for the business. In the past this was what separated the CEO from the floor sweeper. In process-centered organizations they must both be big-picture thinkers; it is just that the CEO's canvas is a broader one.

This style of thinking is an absolute requirement for all jobs in a process-centered organization, but a great many people—perhaps most—have no experience with it. All of us live in boxes of one kind or another. Process centering does away with boxes. How do we learn process thinking? As with almost everything, by doing it. You don't learn a new way of thinking by reading about it. A small business is a good environment for developing one's big-picture faculties. Small companies can't afford the compartmentalization and specialization that cripple our holistic cognitive capabilities. If you can't move to a small company right now, try practicing in your present company. Explore how your work relates to and impacts the work of others. Ask questions (maybe not out loud) that you're not supposed to ask. Where does the information and material that I use come from? Where do the results of my work go? What would happen if I changed this? What would have to be done to make this work twice as fast? What if we suddenly had to do three times as much in the same amount of time? It doesn't matter if you don't come up with the "right" answers. The point of the exercise is to start stretching your mental muscles.

There is another way to develop big-picture thinking skills

that may sound far-fetched to some: learn to program a computer. The logic behind this is that computer programming is nothing but an exercise in systems thinking. Each line of software that you write will interact with each and every other line of software. Unless you develop some big-picture thinking capability, your program will never work. The marvelous thing about a cognitive capability is that it operates across domains; the thinking style that one needs to write and debug a substantial computer program is the same one needed for solving problems in a business process. Once the synapses are put in play they'll snap on anything. But note: Learning the rudiments of computer programming is not the same as "computer literacy," knowing how to operate a personal computer and some popular programs like spreadsheets, word processors, etc. It means learning to use a programming language like C or Pascal or Basic.

Young people have an advantage over the rest of us in not having had their thinking solidified through years of bad habits. Process thinking should eventually be incorporated in secondary and even in elementary school curriculums. This would be inexpensive and easy to do. But at present most college freshmen have little capability in this area. For that reason I urge them to include some engineering in their studies. Engineering is concerned with the design and construction of systems—electronic, mechanical, civil, software, etc. The heart of an engineering education is not learning and applying equations but learning how to create large systems built from small components. Engineering comes to terms with the themes of trade-offs, reliability, performance analysis, complexity, and problem solving—the precise skills that process-centered work demands. Once again, I am not concerned with the content of the discipline but with the cognitive style it requires and engenders. I like the old definition of education: what remains when you forget what you have been taught.

For the process-centered world, an education in process

thinking is essential. However, it is not all that's needed. Process-centered workers must be capable of critical thinking as well. They must know how to ask *why*. A field service rep, an order processor, a product designer, a floor sweeper—anyone working in a process-centered context—must always be asking himself: Why am I doing this? Is this the best way to do it? Am I helping to create value for the customer? Once again, I would submit that critical thinking operates across domains. Once learned in one area it can be applied to virtually any other. To this end, I maintain that there is no better preparation for our technological age than a classical education: By absorbing and confronting the thinking of history's greatest minds, we learn to think for ourselves.

It might seem odd to suggest that the works of Plato and Madison and Joyce prepare one for the twenty-first century, but they are constants in a world of change. Churchill advised people to read Thucydides; he maintained that *The Peloponnesian War* contained all the lessons of history. Wrestling with questions of good and evil, of democracy and justice, of personal and communal responsibilities is a quest without end. But, having engaged in this struggle, one is better prepared to deal with the more mundane, but nonetheless challenging, issues of the workplace.

One particular skill is absolutely required in a process-centered world: communication. Despite the ever-increasing intrusion of technology into our world, human beings remain its key actors. Indeed, as machines take over more of the drone work, uniquely human abilities come to the fore. Process-centered work is interpersonal work. We no longer perform individual tasks in isolation; we perform processes in teams. Teams do not succeed unless they are based on solid mutual understanding. To that end, strong oral and written communication skills are essential. A classical education helps develop these capabilities as well. I often recall advice once offered me by a senior executive at a major pharmaceutical firm, an Englishman with the advantage of a traditional public school education. "All one need learn," he said, "is Latin and computer programming—Latin for communication and programming for thinking." He wasn't far off.

Having maintained that there is no "right" education for the process-centered world, I may seem to contradict myself by recommending one: a double major in computer science and classics. I offer this not because of the conventional wisdom that computers are a fundamental part of the modern workplace. While this is true, it is not relevant to the point I'm making. What one must know about computers in the workplace can be learned in the workplace. Rather it is the systems thinking that lies at the heart of a good computer science curriculum that leads me to recommend it. What one learns in computer science will help in any business context.

But I am not suggesting computer science alone. The point of tempering of the "hard" with the "soft" is to develop capabilities for critical thinking and communications. Or if you don't like my classics and computers suggestion, I have alternatives: electrical engineering and philosophy, or mechanical engineering and medieval history, or aeronautics and theology. Any of these pairs will develop a student's mind for the process-centered era.

If you aspire to a career in the business world, avoid an undergraduate major in business at all costs. You may learn some superficially useful skills, but not the fundamental capabilities needed for the long haul. The great contemporary hazard to real education is premature specialization. To get locked into one set of facts and ideas at an early age—to perfect a narrow expertise—has wounding consequences. There is plenty of time to develop expertise on the job or in a professional school. We all know middle and senior managers who, because they failed to broaden their intellectual bases, couldn't survive in a changing world; we all know engineers with skills made obsolete by the end of the Cold War; and we all know sales reps whose incomes vanished along with the only markets they knew. But learn how to think and you can survive anything.

It's not that process-centered organizations need well-educated ignoramuses. It goes without saying that the sales rep must know how to sell, that the field service rep how to repair, and so on. Skills are and always will be essential. But skills are the easy part. What's new about the process-centered environment is the new cognitive ability it requires.

But avoiding a business degree doesn't mean avoiding a knowledge of business. Quite the contrary. Knowledge of the principles of business, of both business in general and your own business in particular, is an absolute necessity. Cognitive capabilities can't work in a vacuum. An appreciation of the basics of business—the concepts of strategy, cost structure, market economics, cash flow, and capital utilization—must be part of everyone's intellectual capital. You also need to understand the particulars of your own company: its economics; its cost structure; its strengths and weaknesses; its position and direction in the marketplace; its products, customers, and competitors. To accumulate this knowledge, pretend you own the company you work for. Read trade magazines, follow economic reports, act as though you were the one making important decisions. Because, in a sense, you are. Everyone should strive to have the CEO's perspective not only of the company but of its place in its industry and in the larger economy. As "managerial" work and decision making spread throughout the organization, employees must have an appreciation of their context in order to discharge their new responsibilities.

Cognition is left-brain stuff. The right brain, the seat of attitudes and emotions, must also meet the demands of the process-centered environment. As important as doing the job is doing it in the right way. This goes beyond skills and knowledge; it concerns character and attitudes.

Three basic principles must shape the character of an effective process performer. First, you are on your own. No corporate father figure will take care of you. The feudal corporation—managers and workers in a lord-liege relationship—is gone forever. The person that the process-centered organization ultimately cares about is the customer. The company will give you an opportunity, but then it's up to you. Second, take nothing for granted. In a world of constant change, today's certainties are tomorrow's quaint absurdities. The fact that something—a business strategy, a brand, a job, a personal style—was all the rage yesterday means nothing today. Third, no one owes you anything. No one owes you a living, a job, or any guarantee. Long gone is the age when companies provided security, a living for life, steady promotions and raises. The ascendancy of the customer comes at the expense of the worker. Today, you only get what you deserve, and you only deserve what you earn by dint of the value you create.

Character has been defined as what you do when no one is watching. It could also be defined as how you interpret your own story. If you answer "yes" to any of the following questions, you are definitely not yet ready for the process-centered world.

- Do you tend to blame others for your misfortunes?
- Is the phrase "it's not fair" a frequent part of your conversation?
- Do you wait for someone to tell you what to do?
- Are you still coasting on what you learned in school?
- Do you think that you deserve special consideration because of something you did last year?
- Do you feel that you've worked hard and now deserve to take it easy?
- Do you believe that your talents are unappreciated and your contributions unrecognized?
- Do you believe that everything you've accomplished has been by dint of your own efforts alone?
- Do you resent having to break your routine?

- Do you feel that you've worked yourself into a good situation and you're now home free?
- Are you cynical about your organization and what it does for customers?
- Do you resent having to come to work?
- Do you yearn for 5:00 P.M.?

Success in a process-centered organization takes tenacity, self-reliance, and the resilience to cope with change. It's not for whiners and crybabies; it's not for the rigid, for those who can't go with the flow; and it's not for the dependent. You must be willing to take charge of your life and your career. If technology and markets change and your skills become obsolete, you must recognize it's not your company's fault. If it's anybody's fault, it's yours for not having stayed on top of developments and prepared yourself for new challenges. You must believe that yesterday's success does nothing more than entitle you to play the game one more time. You must be committed to nonstop learning, to re-earning your credentials over and over again. You must take to heart the Bible's injunction that "by the sweat of your brow you will eat your bread."

These attitudes must be reflected in behavior. People who recognize that success today does not mean success tomorrow will take care to live below their means. They will realize that they may have to face periods of unstable income. The company may take a sudden downturn, their skills may become suddenly obsolete, or they may decide they need a change or even an entirely new career. You will need a cushion to see you through such periods. Remember that the seven fat years were followed by seven lean ones, and save hard while you can. You must also invest in your own human capital. No longer can you expect to live off the capital (of skills, education, talent) built in early life; it will not pay dividends forever. It is your responsibility to maintain and build your capital reservoir.

Process-centered performers must be mature and responsible adults. They must recognize that there is no magic formula for success; that winning the lottery is a fantasy, not a strategy; that life isn't always the way we want it to be, and rarely is it fair; that we are each ultimately the captains of our own ships. This may not sound like fun, but the rewards of adulthood, while many, do not always include fun.

Many who grew up in the old environment may find it difficult to come to terms with this new paradigm. We all know clock watchers who believe that just showing up and not committing a felony entitles them to a job; corporate politicians who see achieving success as an exercise in currying favor, building empires, and stabbing others in the back; career planners who believe themselves to be on an escalator and can tell you exactly how many days till their next promotion; and complacents who think that old school ties and family background entitle them to a free ride. These people will not thrive or even survive in process-centered companies unless they undergo profound spiritual transformations.

Character is even harder to develop than cognition. By the time we reach adulthood, at least chronological adulthood, our belief systems are largely formed. It usually requires a traumatic event—of the kind that most of us would rather avoid—to reshape our characters. I knew an arrogant and abrasive young man who became wise and perceptive only after he suffered a terrible accident and became a paraplegic. Some require the experience of losing their jobs to face reality. Others mature through force of will, by recognizing in themselves inappropriate attitudes and reactions and working to change them. This is only slighter harder than dieting. For most people it will be a painful transition. As they begin to work in process-centered environments, they will learn through experience that their old attitudes and styles are useless. Most will shed them. Some will not, preferring to wallow in self-pity and resentment. These will have no future.

In closing, let's return to Charles Dickens. In *Great Expectations*, Mr. Wemmick, a solicitor's clerk who has acquired a small fortune in jewels, explains his philosophy of success: "My guiding star always is—Get a hold of portable property." In our process-centered global economy, where job security is an oxymoron, we are all portable property. Your surest path to success is to take control of yourself—your thinking, your education, your skills, your passion, your humanity—and become an adult who can make his or her way anywhere in the world.

CHAPTER 15

PICKING TOMORROW'S WINNERS

AT SOME time in our lives we all have to practice a little security analysis in order to evaluate a company. Maybe we're about to buy a company's product, either for ourselves or for our organization. Nobody wants a computer from a company that won't be around to maintain and upgrade it. Or we may want to invest in a company and, except for day traders, investment represents a bet on a company's staying power and prospects for growth. Or most important, we may be looking at a company as a potential employer. Who wants to board a sinking ship?

Concerns like these are the province of the discipline of security analysis. The great pioneer in this field was Benjamin Graham (1894–1976). Graham was an investor, a Columbia Business School professor, and the author of *The Intelligent*

Investor, published in 1949 and still selling almost half a century later. In 1934 Graham and fellow Columbia professor David Dodd had published *Security Analysis*, which described a system for analyzing a company and predicting its long-term prospects. (A first edition of *Security Analysis* sold for $7,500 in 1994. And one of Graham's protégés, who studied under him at Columbia and then worked at his Wall Street firm, has gone on to do quite well for himself—Warren Buffett.)

A basic Graham tenet is that a company's history foretells its future. A long record of growth in sales, earnings, and dividends indicates that a company will continue to be successful. The foundation of this theory is that consistent financial performance reflects enduring operational strengths, that financial results do not come about by themselves but as byproducts of operational excellence. Graham looked for companies possessed of abundant assets and in a strong financial condition (for instance, book value in excess of stock price), reasoning that these companies had the capability and the resources to do well in the future.

Today, one of Graham's assumptions is out of date. Operations are still the essence and finances the manifestation, but the past no longer predicts the future. The ways of doing business that accounted for past financial success will not necessarily lead to similar results in the future. Indeed, in a world of constant, rapid change, what accounts for yesterday's success may be the very thing that produces tomorrow's failure.

Wang missed the transition to personal computers because its sales force, adept at selling word-processing equipment, could not bear to abandon what was working so well for them. IBM was reluctant to join the swing to end-user computing because of the high profits it enjoyed in selling mainframe computers and peripherals to corporate data centers. The name brands in which consumer-goods companies invest so much equity often become albatrosses when consumers focus on value and low price. Physical assets that can become obsolete overnight are assets in name only.

What worked in the past will work in the future only if the future resembles the past. But the future will not resemble the past. We live in a world of ephemeral product life cycles, of radically changing technology, of unpredictable shifts in consumer taste. Having a well-oiled machine tuned to yesterday guarantees nothing tomorrow.

A company is not just a static collection of assets. It is a system for creating revenues and profits. Once upon a time, perhaps, a company's physical and financial assets were the most important aspects of this system, but no longer. Physical assets can be as much of a drag on a company's future potential as they can be an enabler, and in a world of global capital markets, financial assets are not so scarce nor precious as they once were. The problem of assessing a company remains, but classical security analysis is no longer adequate to the task.

Since the 1960s a popular alternative to Graham's approach has favored growth companies. Modern stock market darlings are young companies that have dominant market share and proprietary technologies. Microsoft, as a consequence, has a larger market capitalization than General Motors, which is more than twenty-five times its size. Netscape, an Internet software company, goes public at $30 a share and within weeks is selling for over $100 a share. Ranging in age from infancy to adolescence, these are not seasoned companies with long track records. But investors are willing to pay high prices for their stocks because they believe that these companies' current strength in developing or even nascent markets will continue as these markets grow. The popularity of these companies, in other words, is based on an unstated premise: that the future, if not an extrapolation of the past, is an extrapolation of the present. But this premise is as dubious as Graham's.

The growth-company dogma assumes that Microsoft's

ownership of today's most popular personal computer software ensures its future market dominance. But the hard fact is that even the strongest contemporary products will not last. For instance, as of this writing there is more and more discussion of the potential demise of the personal computer, which some suggest will be replaced by the "network computer." Such a device would have little computing capacity and would be used primarily to access the Internet and other network-based software systems and databases. It would also come at a very low price. Users of such a device would not purchase software by mail or in a retail store but use network-based software. In this scenario it is far from certain that Microsoft could sustain its present market dominance. Its current control of distribution channels would be irrelevant, along with many of its programs, which are designed for powerful personal computers.

This is not meant to suggest that Microsoft will inevitably fail. The point is that it might. Market dominance today is merely evidence that some wise steps were taken in the past. Once again, what has led to a company's current strength does not guarantee its future strength.

If we can't use financial results or market dominance to assess a company, what can we use? Our first answer, unsurprisingly, is process performance. How well a company performs its processes is the determinant of how well the customer is being served and how inexpensively the company is operating, phenomena that will eventually show up in market share and bottom-line results. So the first thing the modern security analyst should look at is the company's process measures: how fast, accurately, and cheaply does the company develop products, answer customer inquiries, fill orders, and deliver service? We all have to become amateur Baldrige examiners and ISO 9000 certifiers, evaluating a company's processes and its performance. We also have to be sure that the company has a process management system in place dedicated to maintaining its processes and ensuring their continued excellence. This is the best way of assessing the company's current situation, which will manifest itself in tomorrow's results.

But there is a weakness in this approach as well. If my company has better processes than yours, I will outperform you in the market, and if I continue to pay attention to my processes then I can expect to continue to outperform you. However, this will only hold true as long as the market itself doesn't change dramatically. If, however, customers or technologies or industry basics shift radically, then my vaunted processes will suddenly be largely irrelevant. Unfortunately, in today's world, nothing—not financial performance, not market dominance, not even process leadership—can be projected into the future. In an era of lightning-fast change even the best processes can suddenly become more of a liability than an asset, virtually forcing companies to start over. How then can we proceed if neither the past nor the present is a reliable guide to the future?

A model for evaluating companies without resorting to either history or current performance exists in the venture capital industry. Venture capitalists fund infant companies that have little besides talent, concept, and hope. Virtually all venture capitalists follow a guiding principle set forth by the founding father of the American venture capital industry, General Georges Doriot.

Doriot was a World War II general who after the war taught at Harvard Business School and led one of the country's first venture capital firms, American Research and Development. Perhaps his greatest claim to fame is the $70,000 investment he placed with Kenneth Olsen, a young engineer, in 1957, for which his fund received a stake in the company that later became the Digital Equipment Corporation, a stake that was eventually sold for over $400 million.

General Doriot is a legend in the venture capital world. His most famous dictum is the industry's watchword: "I never invest in products or technologies, I only invest in people." At first glance, this seems like a banal cliché. At a second glance, it is astonishing. Not invest in technology or products? Isn't that what venture capitalists do? Aren't start-ups based on technological innovations, breakthrough products, radically new concepts? Isn't the model venture capitalist the farsighted investor who recognizes the potential in the xerographic copier, the personal computer, the discount retailer? The answer to all of these is no. It is nearly impossible for any-one—venture capitalists included—to determine in advance the new products and technologies that will turn out to be winners. Even the personal computer, which with twenty-twenty hindsight was a surefire winner, was anything but that at the time it was being developed. Many people, myself included, thought it was merely a novelty, even a toy. What real applications would it have, we wondered?

This is always the story. The demand for new products and services almost never precedes their invention. With our imag-inations limited by our existing technologies, very few, if any, of us can recognize the real potential of new inventions. Benjamin Franklin's apocryphal remark when asked about the use of a scientific discovery—"What is the use of a newborn baby?"—has universal relevance. Even if a technology works and has real utility, a million imponderables lie between its invention and successful deployment. Moreover, many of the concepts and technologies presented to venture capitalists are simply too complex for them to judge.

In this context General Doriot's statement reveals its true power. He admitted that neither he nor his colleagues were clever enough to predict the success of this technology or that product. But he could tell if the people behind them were tal-ented, aggressive, and ambitious. If the people were winners then there was a good chance their products would be, too.

And if a particular product didn't win, he was sure the people would continue to strive until they came up with one that did. On the other hand, if the people lacked drive and talent then no matter how good their product they would find a way to lose. They would implement poorly, miss the market, or succumb to the competition. Ultimately, said Doriot, it is character rather than concept or technology that determines the destiny of a start-up company.

This character-over-concept principle can also be applied to established companies. At its heart, this perspective maintains that the essence of a company is not what it sells or how it operates, but rather who the company is—its character, culture, personality. Most people would undoubtedly say that some companies win because they develop superior products, excel at manufacturing, and please their customers. Most people would be wrong. Rather, some companies do these things because they are winners to begin with. Action follows character. More than anything else, it is a company's character that determines its prospects for future success. If its people are committed to success, if they have the temperament to withstand adversity and setbacks, if they possess the maturity to know when one path is leading nowhere and recognize that it is time to follow another—then this company, like the start-ups that General Doriot favored, will always find a way to triumph.

Merely doing the right things without having the right spirit avails little, as second-rate companies have learned to their regret. After all, also-rans know what it takes to win as well as the leaders. They know it takes good products, responsive service, and low costs. They can even see how their more successful brethren manage to achieve these desired ends. They try to emulate successful companies, but can't. The reason they fail is that they do not have the character needed to succeed. Eventually character will out and they will find some way to fail. Either their plans will go awry or by the time they approach the pacesetter's level, the pacesetter will have moved on to something else.

It is remarkable how the same handful of companies always seem to win the game no matter how often or quickly the rules change. Companies like GE, 3M, Wal-Mart, Hewlett-Packard, and Motorola have real staying power—and not because they have lucked into some long-lived products or discovered perfect processes. We've seen how fragile these are. Nor is their success the result of tried-and-true ways of doing things. Rather, it's the souls of these organizations that ultimately prevail. And the soul endures no matter how often or quickly the rules change.

In sports it is the same. A team can't count on its star players for long; athletic careers are notoriously brief. Clever plays only work so long as they surprise the opposition. In sports it is the spirit of the franchise that leads to success—both the spirit that inspires players to superior performance and the spirit that prompts the team to attract and recruit the best players, to devise the best strategies, never to let up, and always to find a way to win.

The key to recognizing a successful company is distinguishing genuine superiority from luck. Any company can get lucky, stumbling across that perfectly timed product that breaks sales records for a season, just as even the worst poker player sometimes is dealt an unbeatable hand. But that's quite different from delivering great products year in and year out in the face of changing markets and technologies. For that to happen a company needs a lot more than luck. It needs great processes and the character to find entirely new processes when the old ones no longer suffice. While a company's financial history, operating strengths and weaknesses, customer satisfaction, and product quality do matter and deserve assessment, ultimately the best indicator of long-term performance is the company's character: the one thing that remains constant while all else changes. In other words, the key to assessing a company's long-term strength is evaluating the capabilities of its deep system, as discussed in chapter 13, with special emphasis on values and beliefs, the company's permanent core character.

How can a company's character be assessed? We need measures of corporate heart and soul, ways to determine if the company has the ability to ensure its own renewal. To that end, I offer the following five key themes.

1. *Open inquiry.* Does this company tell the truth? Can it accept unpleasant news and reject conventional wisdom? Are problems relentlessly traced to their real roots, no matter whose ox is gored, or does politics rear its ugly head? Only companies that face reality and admit that the old model is obsolete will create a new one. In too many companies people are afraid to be honest. When the messengers are shot, people soon learn to keep their mouths shut, and disaster is the result. General Electric's Jack Welch nails it when he says, "We must face reality as it is, not as we wish it to be."

The extent of an organization's commitment to truth is indicated by the tenor of its public documents. For example, is the company's annual report just a long set of clichés and platitudes, its problems ascribed to "uncertain markets" and "unanticipated conditions"? Or does it speak plainly and clearly, admitting errors and facing consequences?

2. *Morale.* Do the employees believe in the company or do they suffer from corporate cynicism? Personal performance is never motivated solely by monetary rewards. A pride of belonging and a sense of connection make people dig deep and deliver their personal best. When people care about their organization and fellow workers they are willing to confront unpleasant problems and to take the sometimes wrenching steps needed to correct them.

Cynicism is hard to quantify but easy to recognize. Do people respect senior leadership or is it the object of contempt? Are communications from headquarters dismissed as empty platitudes or taken seriously? Does the mission/vision/values statement mean something or is it just corporate hot air? Do former employees come back to the company? Is there an alumni association? These are signs of high morale. They mark companies where people connect.

3. *Humility.* Is the company arrogant? Do people take their success for granted? Do they behave as if their past triumphs guarantee the future? If so the company will never survive. It will resist change until it is too late, secure in the certainty that it has things right. An organization that will adapt to shifting circumstances is never complacent. As Michael Porter of Harvard Business School puts it, "The best companies are always worried."

When I visit a company whose people are aware of their past success but do not dwell on it, who understand that their current strengths merely position them to compete in the future, then I know I've found a company that has the potential to be around for a long while.

4. *Learning.* Are learning and experimentation organized disciplines in the company or are they haphazard practices? "The learning organization" has become one of the most overused phrases of the 1990s (almost as overused and misused as "reengineering"). Slogans and speeches do not a learning organization make. Explicit policies and processes do. So do institutionalized, measured goals for learning and experimentation. Does the company have such goals? Are managers measured against them? Are funds made available for experiments that may yield extraordinary benefits in the long term or is there only a relentless pursuit of short-term financial results? Is risk tolerated? Is it rewarded? Is a well-managed failure seen as an important learning experience or as a cause for shame? Are the senior managers regarded as people who got where they are by not rocking the boat or by shaking things up? Are mistakes punished or are they examined for

new insights? Have prior efforts for change been successful in the organization? How do such efforts figure in the company's idea of itself? A company's legends are as revealing of its culture as folk tales are of a society's culture. Is an unsuccessful innovation of five years ago now described as a disaster or as an interesting experiment?

5. *Sustainability.* Even if a company scores high on all the foregoing questions—encouraging candor and open inquiry, having high morale and strong employee loyalty, being free of arrogance, and committed to learning and experimentation— one more point must be examined. Are these virtues the creation of one individual or are they an intrinsic part of the organization? Will they last or will they fade?

The nineteenth century saw the rise of the "great man" theory of history, which held that the world was shaped by the actions of powerful individuals. Thomas Carlyle defined history as "the biography of great men." This view has many adherents in the contemporary business world. They see corporations as extensions of the CEO's personality and vision. But a company that is dependent on the greatness of its CEO is a company that will not survive the CEO's departure. It avails the company little in the long term if the CEO manages to instill and enforce the right kind of corporate culture, but only by dint of personality and direct intervention. True leadership is not proven by the exercise of personal charisma. Rather, it is evidenced by the creation of a sustainable environment. If an organization relies on the exploits of one individual then it is in trouble. However, if the leader has created an enduring company character, one that is the very fabric of the company, then the enterprise will endure.

These themes are complex to evaluate. You cannot tell, for instance, if a company is humble or not by inspecting its balance sheet or by conducting a customer survey. Evaluating a company's character requires close scrutiny: meeting the management, talking at length with employees and customers, reading all available materials. This is not easy. But as the effort so the reward; superficial analysis yields superficial understanding. There is no substitute for hard work.

The best way to judge a company is the same way you would judge a person—by what's on the inside, not by what shows. "Clothes do not make the man [or the woman]," nor do any other possessions. Even talent and education, while important, do not guarantee their effective exploitation. We all know high school valedictorians who never fulfilled their potential. What really determines a person's long-term prospects for success is character: work habits, resilience, tenacity, ambition, and willingness to learn. Since a company is at its core a group of people, try to evaluate it in terms of the group personality of these people.

Nations are also groups of peoples, and the same approach can help us ascertain which countries are most likely to thrive in this new economic world. A full treatment of this question lies beyond the scope of this book, but a brief consideration of it is in order.

Why some societies eclipse others has intrigued social scientists for generations. In our time such thinkers as Mancur Olson, Paul Kennedy, and Michael Porter have examined this question from different perspectives and have reached different conclusions. Some answers emphasize societal structure, judging a nation by how well its disparate elements fit together. Others examine the economy to see if its structure creates synergies and advantages in the global context. Perhaps the most popular contemporary view centers on human capital: The key to a strong economy is held to be an educated and willing workforce.

This latter is a valid insight, but it does not go far enough. We must ask a deeper question: *Why* do some countries have better workforces than others? The popular answer is the one favored by many contemporary social scientists. A country will have a better workforce if it invests in the infrastructure that develops human capital, from education to social welfare programs. From this perspective, to be successful a society should build more schools, train more teachers, and pay them higher salaries. This too does not go far enough. Infrastructure by itself does not ensure that human capital will be developed. Many countries spend a lot on infrastructure, but to little avail.

The real strength of a nation lies in its heart, the characteristics of its culture that motivate the kinds of behavior on which economic success is based. Singapore's extraordinary prosperity, for example, is the consequence of a culture that values education, self-reliance, personal responsibility, and deferral of gratification. On the other hand, a society that espouses radical egalitarianism and extreme individualism will have difficulty stimulating cooperation in the workplace, nor will a hedonistic culture encourage the kind of hard work demanded by process-centered companies. In societies that fear dislocation and cherish stability, innovation that inevitably hurts some people in the short run while benefiting all in the long run will be impossible. A culture in which everyone is looking out for number one cannot develop the teamwork that process-centered work requires. This is how the capabilities of a society must be viewed, not in terms of its infrastructure but by its attitudes and values.

Seen through this lens, all the world's major economies have both strengths and weaknesses. Embedded in the American culture is a deep reverence for innovation and entrepreneurship. Our traditional icons are the Yankee inventor, the Silicon Valley entrepreneur, the cowboy, the astronaut, the Arctic explorer. This represents an important advantage. But of late, this current has become muddied. Our new heroes are the sports star, the entertainer, the stock trader, and the pop star—symbols of getting rich quick rather than of creating value. Moreover, we are losing the cohesiveness of our social and civil polity. Always somewhat thin, it is becoming positively frayed. There is less and less of what holds us together, less and less that induces each of us to care about and work for the greater good of the whole. Such a fragmenting environment is not a nourishing one for process-centered work.

Compared to the United States, Europe has a feudal management culture and a weak feel for entrepreneurship. The notions of empowerment and autonomy do not come easily to either managers or frontline workers in most European countries. Strict social and labor regulations impeding change are signs of cultures that long for stability and are willing to sacrifice innovation to achieve it.

Japan's economic strengths are legendary, but its cultural weaknesses are now becoming apparent as well: a preference for consensus over creativity, for gradual rather than radical change. Moreover, if in the United States individualism has gone too far then Japan and some other Asian cultures have erred in the opposite direction. While people in East Asian companies may excel at cooperation and team work, cultural norms there often discourage the kind of open criticism, free inquiry, and useful conflict that generate energy and innovation. If confrontation and losing face are taboo, outdated methods will not be challenged.

All of the world's leading economies—the United States, Western Europe, and Japan—have one significant factor working against them: a history of success. The greatest advantage in the coming years may well lie with emerging economies. These countries and companies have less baggage to dispose of. Some of them may be able to leapfrog over the current leaders into the world of process-centered enterprises. So whether it will be Mexico, Korea, Venezuela, Brazil, or

Malaysia, the place to look for surprises is, as usual, exactly where we least expect to find them.

On every prospectus for a stock offering or mutual fund is a prominent disclaimer: Past results are not a guarantee of future performance. As we enter the process-centered age, this caveat should be writ large—for individuals, for companies, and for countries. It should be emblazoned on the desk and in the heart of every leader, of every employee, and of every citizen.

CHAPTER 16

UTOPIA SOON OR APOCALYPSE NOW?

THE SHAPE of the twenty-first-century company is becoming clear. It will be organized around processes rather than functions. Managers will coach and design rather than supervise and control. Employees will be process performers rather than task workers, with a broad understanding of their process and their company. The company itself will be a dynamic, flexible organization filled with entrepreneurial zeal and focused sharply on customer needs. It will be an organization whose every employee is important, where people are treated as assets, not as expenses. Change will be expected, not feared. Only such a company will be able to provide the extraordinary service, innovation, and low cost essential for success in the new global economy. Companies that cling to traditional hierarchical structures and bureaucratic systems will simply not be able to compete against their process-centered counterparts.

The future belongs to the process-centered organization. But the question remains: Is this a good thing or a bad thing? Business, which creates a society's wealth, shapes society and determines its values. What impact will the process-centered organization have on the larger society? Will this revolution improve the human condition or not? All too often the answers to questions like these are simplistic or ideological. Panglossian optimists assert that all change is for the best, while neo-Luddites are sure that all industrial progress destroys the human spirit. Complex questions cannot be answered with such knee-jerk responses. In reality the process-centered world has both good and bad elements; the best way to describe it is to say that it is very different from what we are accustomed to.

Consider the very core of the process-centered organization: the way people work. As we have said repeatedly throughout this book, process performers are not closely supervised drones. They are self-directed professionals focused on creating customer value. Their work is not industrial era drudgery but a satisfying endeavor that also provides an income.

It is thrilling to be part of a revolution that replaces meaningless work, petty bureaucracy, and dead-end jobs with a workplace to which people enjoy coming, knowing they will be challenged and appreciated. This sunny scenario, however, has a darker side. Process-centered jobs are big jobs with broad range and scope. They require thinking and decision-making. These big jobs require big people to fill them. But what will become of the little people, those who lack the education, the intellectual capacity, or the character to fill the jobs in a process-centered organization?

What will become of the people who merely want to come to work, turn off their brains, and do what they're told until quitting time? Or of those who simply don't have the drive, ambition, and intensity to focus on processes and customers? What of the people who are incapable of big-picture thinking? What of those who can't handle constant change, who need stability and predictability? Must they all be left behind, orphans of the new age?

The cynical reply that the government or the fast food chains will be the employer of last resort is no longer realistic. The fast food restaurants, bargain retailers, service companies, and government organizations that have traditionally sponged up low-level personnel are also becoming process centered and are placing higher demands on their workers. They can't afford the old approaches either. Routine tasks are being automated, and what is left for human beings is exacting and substantive work. The fact is that relegating "low-level" people to "low-level" jobs is no longer an option. Before long, even sweeping the floor will be a big job—involving making decisions, entertaining alternatives, and sharing a sense of personal responsibility.

It would be nice to believe that education and training will bring everyone up to the level required by process-centered jobs. Maybe it's possible, but the prospect of such a dramatic improvement in the American educational system is very doubtful and at best would take many years. The problem of what to do with "little people" will be with us for some time.

There is another wrinkle to the prospect of an economy that offers only big jobs. In the past little jobs have been the entry point into the economy for immigrants and disadvantaged minorities. Low-skill manufacturing or back-office functions offered opportunities to people with little formal education, providing them with a steady wage and the chance to build capital, get a piece of the American dream, and provide a better future for their children. This scenario is closing down. We may be witnessing the birth of an economy with no bottom rungs on the ladder of success.

Are we creating a world in which people are divided into the employable and unemployable—those who have the prospect of exciting, fulfilling careers and those who can't get any job at all? This troubling question is compounded by the implications of the enormous gains in productivity that process-centered organizations are achieving.

The most important measure of business productivity is sales per employee. Companies such as Progressive Insurance and Texas Instruments that have adopted a process-centered philosophy have reported *tripling* this figure in as little as four or five years. It is possible to imagine a future in which only a small number of people are required to produce all the goods and services that a society currently consumes. In such a world how will the rest of us survive? Dramatic increases in productivity are not intrinsically bad. On the contrary, they are very good. They are the only real engine for raising the standard of living. History teaches us that human demand is virtually infinite. Whenever a major advance in productivity allows fewer people to produce the goods and services an economy consumes, the eventual result is not massive unemployment but rather a flowering of new goods and services to satisfy previously unmet and even unrecognized appetites. But there remains a question of timing. It takes some time to identify the new goods and services that people want and to organize the new enterprises that will produce them. Can that be done fast enough to absorb the legions of workers (both those already in the workforce and newcomers) who will no longer be required by existing enterprises?

Some suggest that we should change working conditions to compensate for increased productivity. Shorter work weeks and longer vacations would enable more people to have jobs, earn an income, and thereby be in a position to consume.

However, there are two basic flaws in this simplistic argument. Shorter work weeks raise a company's costs by making it pay more people than it needs to do the work. So long as all companies do this, none suffers a competitive disadvantage. But if some companies don't go along, those who do are burdened with higher costs and will not survive. Labor laws and regulations to ensure the implementation of such policies only apply within the regulating country. In a free world economy there will always be people somewhere willing to work harder and longer for less pay, thereby enabling their employers to offer equivalent products and services at lower costs. In the long run customers will not support paying two people to do a job that one could do.

The second flaw in this argument is less economic and more psychological. If people only work twenty or twenty-five hours a week, what will they do with the rest of their time? Americans have not shown themselves to be particularly inventive at filling their leisure hours. The prospect that process centering will lead to people spending more hours in front of a television set (even an interactive one) absorbing mindless nonsense is not an uplifting one. Moreover, the need to work—to strive, to achieve, to excel—is deep-seated in the human psyche. Limiting people's capacity to achieve is a very questionable strategy.

Process centering may also have some subtle effects on the larger structure of an economy. One of the virtues of process centering is that it makes large organizations nimble and flexible. No longer lumbering giants wedded to the past, they can respond quickly, even proactively, to market conditions and customer needs. But if the elephants are dancing, what will become of the mice?

Historically, aggressive start-up companies have been one of the major fountains of innovation and employment in the American economy. The brash newcomer that seizes an opportunity before its larger competitors even know it's there is a staple of American business history. Sharp eyes and high energy may be the only competitive advantages that start-up companies have. By all rational considerations Wal-Mart should never have overtaken Sears. The older retailer had every imaginable edge—a universally recognized brand name, stores throughout the country, a relationship with most American households, and very deep pockets. However, its inflexible bureaucracy slowed it down to the point where Wal-Mart overtook it. A vigorous, process-centered Sears would never have allowed that. Moving forward, will a reborn Sears and an ever-innovative Wal-Mart preempt others from exploiting new opportunities? Is there hope for the Wal-Marts of the future or are we condemning ourselves to an economy dominated by established giants?

Process centering is in an important way a by-product of a free global economy. A world marketplace of intense competition and customer power demands that companies attend to their processes so as to be as efficient and responsive as possible. But, as we have been saying, there are drawbacks to the new regime: Some people's lives will be dislocated, some vested interests will be disturbed, a new style of intensity and dynamism will rudely replace one of complacency and continuity. These consequences may provoke a backlash against reengineering, process centering, and the global economy that gave them birth. An early harbinger of this was the opposition to NAFTA and GATT in the United States. More recently, we have witnessed the demonization of corporate leaders, a flood of magazine articles about the tragedy of downsizing, and dark mutterings about punishing companies that don't guarantee their employees a secure future. If this keeps up, we may see a resurgence of tariffs and protectionism, or a new wave of isolationist legislation that masquerades as pro-labor policy or as limitations on capital flows and technology transfers. Economists of every ideological stripe agree that free markets benefit everyone and that restrictions on global trade are undesirable, unsustainable, and nearly impossible to enforce. But just because an idea is very bad does not mean it will be unpopular. Process centering may represent the fruition of the global economy or it may be the phenomenon that leads to its breakdown.

Process centering will also reshape the values of our society, but whether for good or ill it is too soon to say. One of the strengths of process-centered work is that, by focusing on objective process measures, it strips people of false status. All that matters is how you perform and the results you achieve. Connections, background, ethnicity, race, religion, and gender no longer count. The process-centered organization is a true meritocracy, the original American ideal and the realization of Dr. Martin Luther King's dream that men and women be judged only by the content of their character.

On the other hand, the process-centered organization may turn into a nightmare. It may foster a brutal form of social Darwinism and a perverse modern Calvinism. When we focus so resolutely on business performance, it can become the single lens through which others see us—and through which we see ourselves. Only those who succeed may come to be viewed as worthwhile (even by themselves). The successful may become repulsively self-congratulatory, while others may look into the mirror and feel ashamed.

It may also become confusing and disorienting to work and live in a process-centered world. As we have said, a process-centered organization is dedicated to the proposition that the more things change, the less they stay the same. It is ready, able, and eager to abandon yesterday's success in pursuit of new challenges and new markets.

While such dedication to the future is commendable and economically rational, it may also mean a loss of tradition, a separation of people and organizations from their pasts. The future is where we will have to live, but the past makes it livable. It is tradition, after all, that gives us a sense of community and continuity.

Without a connection to the past, we may become rootless, ruthless, and alienated. Will a hunger for change produce a permanent condition of future shock? Will we face spiritual poverty even as we enjoy material plenty? Will never-ending organizational improvement inevitably produce a culture of tension and stress? Will it destroy our very humanity? Will intense concentration on customer demands usurp attention to family and community? Will we become a society of maximally efficient workers who never stop to smell the roses, for whom beauty, art, and religion mean nothing? Is the text for the process-centered world Aldous Huxley's *Brave New World*, that frightening vision of a completely "rational" society, or is it *Lost Horizon*, James Hilton's wistful account of Shangri-la, the perfect human society?

Let us be clear about one thing. Whether boon or bane, the process-centered world is at our doorstep. It is the inevitable result of technological advances and global market changes. The question that we must confront is not whether to accept it but what we make of it.

I can offer no facile answers, no easy solutions, to these questions. Addressing these problems is far beyond one person's capacity. It will require the active engagement and contribution of all sectors of our society. The first responsibility of those of us who are helping to usher in this new age is to make others aware of what is happening, of both its potentials and its shortcomings. We must begin to make ourselves heard, to direct our concerns to opinion leaders and politicans, to the media, and to all our fellow citizens. This will be no small task. While we are undergoing the most important economic transformation since the Industrial Revolution, little attention is being paid outside the business world to the issues raised in this chapter. Our whole society seems obsessed instead with transient and even trivial political and cultural issues.

There is one other thing we can do to help cushion the impact of the transition to the process-centered world: We can adjust our expectations. Process centering is neither all good nor all bad; like everything else in life, it is a mixed bag. Whether it is seen as mostly good or mostly bad depends on who is doing the seeing. Our new world will be very different from the one to which we are accustomed, and no one likes letting go of the familiar. It will be all too easy for people to forget the rigidity of function-based organizations, the degrading nature of supervisory management, the flaws of bureaucracies—particularly when confronted with the complexities and discomforts of the transition. There is no stronger evidence of the human propensity to romanticize the past than the resurgence of the Communist party in Russia and Eastern Europe. We will all have to accept that the past is gone, that the security and continuity that the old world offered were purchased at a very stiff price, and that in an important sense they were illusions to begin with. If we regard the process-centered future as inevitable and address it with courage, we will then make the best that can be made of it.

I submit, however, that process-centered organizations do deliver one unqualified good—not for customers or investors but for the people who work in them. They give us a new reason to work—a new reason that is also among the very oldest.

The wages of work can be paid in a variety of currencies. The most basic is, of course, monetary. We work to earn a living for ourselves and our families. If we are lucky, we can also derive feelings of satisfaction, accomplishment, and pride from a job well done. Some of us are even granted the joy of excitement and stimulation that comes from interesting and challenging work. But there is another reward that we reap all too rarely today. We need our work to have transcendent meaning, but it rarely does.

We all periodically ask ourselves late at night, "What's it all for?" Work is the dominant concern of most of our waking hours. Is there nothing more to it than earning money and experiencing the occasional burst of adrenaline? Is work just about accumulating possessions? Is there no larger point to our lives? Money becomes dross and excitement pales if we do not believe that there is some deeper meaning and value to our work, something about it that takes us beyond our own narrow concerns. To quote Hillel, the first-century Talmudic sage, "If I am not for myself, who will be for me? But if I am just for myself, what am I?"

Our premodern ancestors did not suffer from this dilemma. While their material lives were incomparably poorer than ours, their spiritual lives were far richer. They believed that there was an abiding purpose to their labors: the service of the Eternal. Religion was a universal component of people's lives. In religious life, work was not just seen as an economic activity or a mode of personal expression. It was a form of devotion. In monasteries and convents of many orders and many faiths, initiates performed work not for financial but for spiritual rewards. In classical Hebrew the same word denotes both religious worship and daily work.

Work should give substance, meaning, and value to our lives. It should make us feel that we are contributing to the world, that we are helping to make it a better place, that we are somehow leaving a legacy. Work should help us focus not on ourselves but on others, the beneficiaries of our work, and, in so doing, free us from the relentless focus on our own concerns that eventually leaves the taste of ashes in our mouths.

Industrial Age work rarely satisfied these abiding needs because the Industrial Age forced us to strike a Faustian bargain. In return for higher wages and an improved standard of living we largely sacrificed the benefits to the spirit that preindustrial work provided. How could it be otherwise? By focusing on isolated and atomistic tasks, by disconnecting people from the end products and customers of their labors, modern work squeezed all sense of transcendent value out of people's lives. It is difficult to take spiritual nourishment from processing a piece of paper or tightening bolts day in and day out. Without a sense of where your product goes or why you are making it, it is hard for your work to mean anything. It is empty, a mechanical ritual performed for transitory reasons.

Process centering changes all this. Your work may still largely consist of tightening bolts or handling forms, but you now have a sense of control and influence over it. You are a responsible actor in your own work drama; you make choices and you make a difference. No longer a blind automaton carrying out preprogrammed instructions, you have become a professional. The original definition of "profession," according to the *Oxford English Dictionary*, was "the declaration or vow made by a person entering a religious order, or the action of entering a religious order." The first professionals were medieval monks and nuns. Modern professionals share with them a sense that work has meaning beyond the purely economic.

The recent spate of books and seminars on "workplace spirituality," despite their often superficial and sometimes ludicrous content, bespeaks a longing for transcendent meaning in our daily lives. In our secular age we may no longer see our work as service to the Divine, but we can see it as service to humanity. It is in this sense that John Martin, CEO of Taco Bell, tells his people that serving the customer "has nobility." Serving the customer is not a mechanical act but one that provides an opportunity for fulfillment and meaning.

Even the most mundane work can be given meaning and value for those who perform it if they understand how it benefits, even in the simplest of ways, the lives of others. Process-centered work can help satisfy everyone's hunger for connection with something beyond themselves and their own needs. It widens our horizons and connects us with others—with our teammates, with our organization, with our customers. In the process-centered world dignity is restored to work, the dignity that was lost to workers who only performed repetitive tasks.

Pope John Paul II has written in a papal encyclical, "Through work, man achieves fulfillment as a human being. Man shares by his work in the activity of the Creator." These prophetic words capture the essence of process-centered work. By making them a reality, the twenty-first-century organization will truly be on the side of the angels.

INDEX